SOLICITORS ACCOUNTS

The University of Law

SOLICITORS ACCOUNTS

FIFTH EDITION

Jacqueline Kempton

This edition published 2025 by

The University of Law
2 Bunhill Row
London EC1Y 8HQ

British Library Cataloguing in Publication Data

A catalogue record for this book is available from the British Library.

ISBN 978 1 80502 261 9

Preface

This book is part of a series of Study Manuals that have been specially designed to support the reader to achieve the SQE1 Assessment Specification in relation to Functioning Legal Knowledge. Each Study Manual aims to provide the reader with a solid knowledge and understanding of fundamental legal principles and rules, including how those principles and rules might be applied in practice.

This Study Manual covers the Solicitors Regulation Authority's syllabus for the SQE1 assessment for Solicitors Accounts in a concise and tightly focused manner. The Manual provides a clear statement of relevant legal rules and a well-defined road map through examinable law and practice. The Manual aims to bring the law and practice to life through the use of example scenarios based on realistic client-based problems and allows the reader to test their knowledge and understanding through single best answer questions that have been modelled on the SRA's sample assessment questions.

For those readers who are students at the University of Law, the Study Manual is used alongside other learning resources and the University's assessment bank to best prepare students not only for the SQE1 assessments, but also for a future life in professional legal practice.

We hope that you find the Study Manual supportive of your preparation for SQE1 and we wish you every success.

The legal principles and rules contained within this Manual are stated as at 1 May 2025.

Author acknowledgments
The writer would like to thank Professor Lesley King for her generous and invaluable help in the preparation of this Manual.

Contents

Table of Cases

Table of Legislation, Codes and Rules

1 Double Entry Bookkeeping and the SRA Accounts Rules

SQE1 syllabus

This chapter will help you to achieve the SQE1 Assessment Specification in relation to Functioning Legal Knowledge by introducing you to the core principles of double entry bookkeeping and the SRA Accounts Rules.

Note that for SQE1, candidates are not usually required to recall specific case names or cite statutory or regulatory authorities. Cases are provided for illustrative purposes only.

Learning outcomes

By the end of this chapter you will be able to apply relevant core principles of double entry bookkeeping and the SRA Accounts Rules appropriately and effectively, at the level of a competent newly qualified solicitor in practice, to realistic client-based ethical problems and situations in the following areas:

- The rules which underlie double entry bookkeeping;
- The basic accounting entries required using the double entry system;
- The principles governing the SRA Accounts Rules and who is bound by them.

1.1 Introduction

All businesses need to keep records of their financial dealings. Law firms are no exception. Those running the firm need to be able to keep track of its financial position: whether the firm is making a profit or can afford to take on more staff, for example.

The term 'accounts' is used to describe the day-to-day records which a firm keeps of its financial transactions. The financial dealings of law firms are generally quite complex. So many different events occur that it is impractical for those running the firm to rely on individual documents, such as bank statements and client bills, to provide a full picture of the firm's financial position. Instead it is necessary for the relevant information to be taken from the individual documents and entered on separate records. These separate records, or accounts, are therefore simply summaries of financial information.

All law firms, from sole practitioners to multinational LLPs, follow the same standard process for recording financial transactions in their accounts.

Law firms differ from many other types of business in that they often hold money which belongs to other people, typically the firm's clients. The public at large must be able to place trust and confidence in law firms to deal with such money appropriately. As a matter of professional conduct, solicitors must therefore adhere to rules on the proper handling of clients' money and the keeping of accounting records.

This chapter looks at:

- double entry bookkeeping;
- the form of accounts;
- making accounting entries;
- cash and ledger accounts;
- SRA Accounts Rules.

1.2 Double entry bookkeeping

The process of recording financial transactions in the accounts of a law firm is called bookkeeping. This terminology harks back to the days when these records were hand-written, or 'entered', into large bound books; and indeed, these day-to-day records are often referred to as 'the books' of the business. Today, of course, firms usually keep their financial records using computerised systems.

All firms use the same bookkeeping system to record their day-to-day transactions. This system is called the double entry bookkeeping system. The system is not unique to law firms and is in fact used as standard by businesses of all types and sizes throughout the world. The double entry system was developed in the fifteenth century by Venetian traders. The fact that it continues to be used today is a tribute to their ingenuity and its efficiency.

Double entry bookkeeping is a system of recording financial dealings built upon a series of rules. Some of the rules may appear arbitrary or perhaps even counter-intuitive. The fact is that the Venetian traders could have decided to set up the whole system differently, but they chose not to. However, once that initial decision is accepted, the system develops its own internal logic.

1.2.1 Principles of double entry

Double entry bookkeeping is based on the premise that every financial transaction has two aspects to it and both aspects need to be recorded. The following examples illustrate the two aspects of a number of transactions:

(a) The firm pays cash to buy premises:

Aspect 1 - The firm has less cash

Aspect 2 - The firm has acquired an asset in the form of premises

(b) The firm pays staff wages:

Aspect 1 - The firm has less cash

Aspect 2 - The firm has incurred an expense

(c) The firm bills a client for work done:

Aspect 1 - The firm has earned income

Aspect 2 - The firm has a debt (the amount of the bill) owing to it

(d) The client pays the firm the money owed:

Aspect 1 - The firm has lost the debt that was owing to it

Aspect 2 - The firm has more cash

Both aspects of a transaction are recorded in the books. Each aspect must be recorded in a different account. The double entry bookkeeping system requires the firm to have a number of separate accounts, so, for example, there is one account for cash, one account for each type of asset, one for each type of expense, one for each person to whom the firm owes money, one for each debtor that owes money to the firm.

In order to record the two aspects, accounts are divided into two sides. The two aspects of any transaction are recorded on different sides of the two accounts.

1.2.2 Rules for recording transactions

The rules for recording transactions are summarised in the following table:

Left column	**Right column**
Expense incurred	Income earned
Asset acquired/increased	Asset disposed of/reduced
Liability reduced/extinguished	Liability incurred/increased
Cash gained	Cash paid

Every transaction has two aspects. When an individual transaction is recorded, one aspect appears in the left-hand column of the grid and will therefore be recorded on the left-hand side of one account. The other aspect appears in the right-hand column of the grid and will therefore be recorded on the right-hand side of another account. For every transaction these two aspects must first be identified and then each of them recorded in two separate accounts.

Example

(a) A firm buys office furniture for £20,000 cash.

Expense incurred	Income earned
Asset acquired/increased	Asset disposed of/reduced
Liability reduced/extinguished	Liability incurred/increased
Cash gained	Cash paid

The firm gains an asset in the form of the furniture (recorded on the left of the office furniture account) and pays cash (recorded on the right of the cash account).

(b) A firm rents out part of its premises. The tenant pays the monthly rent.

Expense incurred	Income earned
Asset acquired/increased	Asset disposed of/reduced
Liability reduced/extinguished	Liability incurred/increased
Cash gained	Cash paid

Rent received is a form of income for the firm. The firm earns income (recorded on the right of the rent account); there is a gain of cash (recorded on the left of the cash account).

(c) A firm pays its electricity bill.

Expense incurred	Income earned
Asset acquired/increased	Asset disposed of/reduced
Liability reduced/extinguished	Liability incurred/increased
Cash gained	Cash paid

Electricity is an expense of the firm. The firm incurs an expense (recorded on the left of the electricity account); there is a payment of cash (recorded on the right of the cash account).

Using the double entry system transactions are simply recorded as they occur. The system is a mechanical method of recording transactions as they happen and involves no value judgements about the state of the business – for example, whether it is making a profit.

1.2.3 The business owner

Another important principle of double entry bookkeeping is that the business is regarded as completely separate from its owner or proprietor. So, when a proprietor sets up a business and puts in some cash, the transaction must be recorded from the point of view of the business. The two aspects of the transaction are that the business is gaining cash and is incurring a liability, in that it now owes money to the proprietor. This liability to repay its proprietor is normally referred to as the 'capital' of the business.

1.2.4 Debit and credit

The double entry system uses the labels 'Debit' and 'Credit' for the two sides of the accounts. 'Debit' is used as a label for the left-hand side and 'Credit' as a label for the right-hand side. They are usually shortened to 'DR' and 'CR' respectively.

Example

A firm buys a photocopier for £5,000.

The firm pays cash (recorded on the right of the cash account with a CR entry) and gains an asset in the form of the photocopier (recorded on the left of the photocopier account with a DR entry).

1.3 The form of accounts

Accounts may be presented in a variety of different forms. The most common is the tabular form:

Name of Account				
Date	**Details**	**DR**	**CR**	**Balance**

When the transaction is recorded, the date of the transaction is entered in the 'Date' column. The 'Details' column contains a cross-reference to the name of the account where the other part of the double entry is made, often with a brief description of the nature of the transaction as well. The amount involved is entered in the left-hand debit column (DR) or the right-hand credit column (CR), as appropriate. The 'Balance' column shows the running balance on the account. If the DR entries exceed the CR entries, the balance is described as a DR balance, and vice versa.

Example

A firm pays three electricity bills: £1,000, £2,000 and £3,000. Each payment will be recorded on the electricity account and the cash account. The electricity account will show debit entries as the business is incurring an expense:

Electricity				
Date	**Details**	**DR**	**CR**	**Balance**
1	Cash	1,000		1,000DR
2	Cash	2,000		3,000DR
3	Cash	3,000		6,000DR

The corresponding entries appear in the cash account as credit entries because the business is paying cash:

Cash				
Date	**Details**	**DR**	**CR**	**Balance**
1	Electricity		1,000	1,000CR
2	Electricity		2,000	3,000CR
3	Electricity		3,000	6,000CR

1.4 Making entries

Using the double entry system, every financial transaction must be recorded in the accounts of the business as it happens. The following example shows how the entries are made to record a series of simple transactions which may typically occur in the early stages of the life of a business.

Example

Miriam, a solicitor, sets up a business as a sole practitioner.

The following financial transactions occur:

June

1 *Miriam starts the business and puts in £10,000 cash*

2 *Business buys a computer for £2,000*

4 *Business pays rent of £1,000*

To record these events the business will need the following accounts:

- *a capital account*
- *a cash account*
- *an asset account for the computer*
- *an expense account for rent*

The following entries are required in the accounts of the business:

1 June Miriam puts in £10,000 cash

The two aspects of this transaction are that the business:

- *gains cash*
- *incurs a liability to Miriam*

There will be a DR entry on the cash account and a CR entry on the capital account:

Cash				
Date	**Details**	**DR**	**CR**	**Balance**
1 June	Capital	10,000		10,000DR

Capital				
Date	**Details**	**DR**	**CR**	**Balance**
1 June	Cash		10,000	10,000CR

2 June Business buys a computer for £2,000

The two aspects to this transaction are that the business:

- *pays cash*
- *gains an asset*

There will be a CR entry on the cash account and a DR entry on the computer account:

Cash				
Date	**Details**	**DR**	**CR**	**Balance**
1 June	Capital	10,000		10,000DR
2 June	**Computer**		**2,000**	**8,000DR**

Computer				
Date	**Details**	**DR**	**CR**	**Balance**
2 June	Cash	2,000		2,000DR

4 June Business pays rent of £1,000

The two aspects of this transaction are that the business:

- *pays cash*
- *incurs an expense*

There will be a CR entry on the cash account and a DR entry on the expense account for rent:

Cash				
Date	**Details**	**DR**	**CR**	**Balance**
1 June	Capital	10,000		10,000DR
2 June	Computer		2,000	8,000DR
4 June	**Rent**		**1,000**	**7,000DR**

Rent				
Date	**Details**	**DR**	**CR**	**Balance**
4 June	**Cash**	**1000**		**1,000DR**

In due course in the above example the business will generate income by charging the clients for the work Miriam has done on their behalf. When a bill is issued, a solicitor will need to record the two aspects of the transaction. The first aspect is the sale of the solicitor's services and the second aspect is the gain of the debt now owed by the client to the firm. Charges for professional services are recorded as a CR entry on an income account, often called 'profit costs'. The client's debt is recorded as a DR entry on an account in the name of the client. When the client eventually pays, the solicitor will record a receipt of cash and the loss of the debt owed by the client to the firm. It is important to notice that no entry is made on the profit costs account when the client pays the cash due. The profit costs account merely records the bill issued. It does not show whether or not clients have paid their bills.

1.5 Cash and ledger accounts

A large number of transactions have one aspect which will be recorded in the cash account. Most firms operate by banking all receipts and making virtually all payments by electronic means or cheque. The so-called 'cash' account (sometimes referred to as the 'cash sheet' or 'cash book') is in reality a record of receipts into and payments out of the bank account. However, a firm will usually need a small amount of cash in the office to cover small, day-to-day expenses. This is referred to as 'petty cash'. A petty cash account is required to record the periodic receipts of cash from the bank and the various payments made from petty cash.

Traditionally, accounts were kept together in a bound book referred to as the 'ledger'. The cash account was the busiest account and was kept in a separate book. This distinction is of no practical importance, as accounts are now usually computerised. However, it makes a difference in terminology, since all the accounts are referred to as 'ledger accounts' apart from the cash account and, where there is one, the petty cash account.

1.6 SRA Accounts Rules

A law firm, like any business, needs to keep day-to-day records of its financial dealings. In common with other business, law firms make those records using the double entry bookkeeping system. However, what distinguishes law firms from most other businesses is that law firms frequently hold money that belongs to other people. For example, clients who are buying property or a business will normally give funds to their solicitor in advance of completion of the purchase. Solicitors are subject to strict rules about dealing with clients' money imposed by the Solicitors Regulation Authority: the SRA Accounts Rules ('the Rules').

1.6.1 The nature of the Rules

In essence the purpose of the Rules is to ensure that money belonging to clients is safe and kept separately from money belonging to the firm. The Rules are designed to reduce the risk of accidental or deliberate misuse of clients' money, and to protect clients from the risks of accidental or deliberate mishandling of their money.

The Rules are principle based and outcome focused. Consequently, in many instances it is left to individual firms to interpret the Rules and apply them in an appropriate and justifiable manner to their own business practices. Therefore, although the Rules provide a framework, firms should also have their own policies and procedures in place to add the detail. However, the Rules also adopt a risk-based approach, becoming more prescriptive in those areas where the risk to clients' money is higher.

The Rules form part of the SRA Standards and Regulations. Breach of the Rules is a disciplinary matter which may result in the SRA taking action against individuals and/or firms in accordance with its Enforcement Strategy. The SRA takes a proportionate approach to disciplinary matters, focusing on substantive rather than trivial or technical breaches. It is clear from the Enforcement Strategy that the SRA regards misconduct involving dishonesty or the misuse of clients' money as serious.

The Rules are supported by online Guidance issued by the SRA from time to time.

The current Rules came into effect on 25 November 2019. The SRA's stated intention in introducing the Rules in this form was to focus on key principles and requirements for keeping client money safe, including:

(i) keeping client money separate from the firm's own money;

(ii) ensuring client money is returned promptly at the end of a matter;

(iii) using client money only for its intended purpose; and

(iv) proportionate requirements for firms to obtain an annual accountant's report.

Changes to the Rules may be imminent. In February 2025, the SRA concluded a consultation, 'Client money in legal services'. Among the issues explored in the consultation is whether it is necessary or desirable for firms to hold client money as widely as now or at all.

1.6.2 Principles governing the Rules

The SRA Standards and Regulations include the SRA Principles. These Principles define the fundamental ethical and professional standards that the SRA expects of all firms and individuals it regulates. The Principles apply to all aspects of practice, including the regulation of Accounts. The Principles are as follows:

You act:

1. in a way that upholds the constitutional principle of the rule of law, and the proper administration of justice;
2. in a way that upholds public trust and confidence in the solicitors' profession and in legal services provided by authorised persons;
3. with independence;
4. with honesty;
5. with integrity;
6. in a way that encourages equality, diversity and inclusion;
7. in the best interests of each client.

The SRA Standards and Regulation includes a Glossary comprising a set of defined terms.

1.6.3 Who is bound by the Rules?

Rule 1 states that the Rules apply to authorised bodies, their managers and employees, and references to 'you' in the Rules should be read accordingly. (Authorisation in this context refers to being authorised by the SRA to, essentially, carry out most types of legal work and so the term 'authorised body' will encompass most firms of solicitors and sole practitioners.) The authorised body's managers are jointly and severally responsible for compliance with the Rules by the authorised body, its managers and employees.

Weston v The Law Society *(1998) The Times, 15 July*
This case illustrates the significance of the Rules and the importance of compliance. The Court of Appeal confirmed that it was appropriate to strike off a solicitor where no dishonesty was alleged against him. The solicitor in question was held to be liable for breaches of the Rules committed by his fellow partners even though he had been unaware of them. Lord Bingham of Cornhill referred to the 'duty of anyone holding anyone else's money to exercise a proper stewardship in relation to it'.

Summary

- Law firms use the double entry bookkeeping system when recording day-to-day transactions.
- The double entry bookkeeping system recognises that every financial transaction has two aspects. Each aspect is recorded on an account. There will be one DR entry and one CR entry for each transaction.
- All firms authorised by the SRA (including the individuals who manage or work within them) must comply with the SRA Accounts Rules.
- The SRA Accounts Rules impose strict requirements on the handling of clients' money and the keeping of accounting records.

Sample questions

Question 1

A firm of solicitors makes a number of cash payments over the course of a month.

For which of the following cash payments would the corresponding double entry reflect the fact that the firm has incurred an expense?

A £100,000 for staff wages.

B £15,000 to buy a photocopier.

C £20,000 for new office furniture.

D £50,000 in repayment of a bank loan.

E £3,000 to buy a computer.

Answer

Option A is correct. Staff wages are part of the outgoings or running costs of the business and it is therefore an expense of the firm.

The other options are wrong. In options B, C and E the payment of cash results in the firm acquiring something which is a long-term benefit - the firm has gained an asset. In option D the firm has reduced a liability.

Question 2

A firm of solicitors buys new office premises for £1 million.

Which of the following pair of double entries shows how the transaction should be recorded?

A CR entry Cash account. DR entry Premises account.

B CR entry Cash account. DR entry Capital account.

C CR entry Premises account. DR entry Cash account.

D CR entry Cash account. DR entry Expense account.

E CR entry Expense account. DR entry Premises account.

Answer

Option A is correct. The two aspects of the transaction are that the firm loses cash and gains an asset in the form of the office premises. This is recorded by a CR entry on the cash account and a DR entry on the Premises account.

Question 3

A firm of solicitors issues a bill to a client for its professional charges. The firm correctly records the debt now owed to the firm by making a DR entry in a client account in the name of the client.

Which of the following best explains how the corresponding double entry should be recorded?

A A DR entry on the Profit costs account because the firm has earned income.

B A DR entry on the Cash account because the firm has gained cash.

C A CR entry on the Profit costs account because the firm has earned income.

D A CR entry on the Profit costs account because the firm has incurred a liability.

E A CR entry on an Expense account because the firm has incurred an expense.

Answer

Option C is correct. The corresponding entry to a DR must be a CR (with the result that options A and B must be wrong). The sale of the solicitor's services is recorded as a CR entry on an income account, often called 'Profit costs', to show that the firm has earned income (options D and E are wrong in that the sale of the solicitor's services is neither a liability nor an expense). The firm will not record any receipt of cash until the bill is paid.

2 Client Money and Client Accounts

SQE1 syllabus

This chapter will enable you to achieve the SQE1 Assessment Specification in relation to Functioning Legal Knowledge concerned with the core principles of double entry bookkeeping and the SRA Accounts Rules on:

- definition of client money;
- requirement to pay client money into a client account;
- circumstances in which money may be withdrawn from a client account;
- repayment of client money;
- meaning and name of a client account;
- obligation not to use client account to provide banking facilities;
- requirement to keep client money separate from money belonging to the authorised body;
- requirement to keep and maintain accurate records.

Note that for SQE1, candidates are not usually required to recall specific case names or cite statutory or regulatory authorities. Cases are provided for illustrative purposes only.

Learning outcomes

By the end of this chapter you will be able to apply relevant core principles of double entry bookkeeping and the SRA Accounts Rules appropriately and effectively, at the level of a competent newly qualified solicitor in practice, to realistic client-based ethical problems and situations in the following areas:

- Distinguishing client money from the firm's own money;
- Identifying what money can or must pass through the client bank account;
- Permitted dealings with client money;
- Protecting client money;
- Accounting records relating to client money.

2.1 Introduction

The concept of client money is central to the Rules. It is this money that the Rules are intended to protect. Part 2 of the Rules defines client money, details what can and cannot be done with such money and sets out the accounting systems and controls that a firm must have in place to protect client money.

This chapter looks at:

- client money;
- client accounts;
- paying money into the client bank account;
- returning client money;
- keeping client money separate from the firm's own money;
- withdrawal of client money from the client bank account;
- improper use of a client bank account as a banking facility;
- client accounting systems and controls.

2.2 Client money

Rules 2–4 set out what an authorised body (for ease of reference, 'a firm') must do with client money as defined in Rule 2.1.

Rule 4.1 requires client money to be kept separate from the money belonging to the firm (usually in a separate client bank account). Beyond that, no requirements are imposed on what the firm does with its own money. The firm will, of course, choose to operate one or more bank accounts for its own money, referred to as 'business' bank accounts.

'Client' is defined in the Glossary as 'the person for whom you act'. However, the definition of client money goes beyond the holding of money for a client.

Rule 2.1 states that client money is money held or received by a firm:

(a) relating to regulated services delivered by you to a client;

(b) on behalf of a third party in relation to regulated services delivered by you (such as money held as agent, stakeholder or held to the sender's order);

(c) as a trustee or as the holder of a specified office or appointment, such as donee of a power of attorney, Court of Protection deputy or trustee of an occupational pension scheme;

(d) in respect of your fees and any unpaid disbursements if held or received prior to delivery of a bill for the same.

Rule 2.1(b) and (c) extends the meaning of client money considerably. Note, for example, that money held to sender's order is client money (and its receipt must be recorded on a separate ledger in the sender's name). In *Challinor and Others v Juliet Bellis & Co and Another* [2013] EWHC 347 (Ch), Hildyard J made the point that a solicitor has a duty to clarify any ambiguity as to whom client money is held for.

'Fees' are defined in the Glossary as 'your own charges or profit costs (including any VAT element)'. 'Disbursements' are defined in the Glossary as 'any costs or expenses paid or to be paid to a third party on behalf of the client or trust (including any VAT element) save for office expenses such as postage and courier fees'. The word 'costs' is defined as 'fees and disbursements' and so covers both.

The effect of Rule 2.1(d) is that money received for all fees and disbursements paid to the firm is considered client money unless and until billed. Such receipts must therefore be held in a client bank account (unless they are the only categories of client money held by the firm and the firm takes advantage of the exemption in Rule 2.2 - see below). Such money is often referred to as money 'generally on account of costs'. Its use is dealt with under Rule 4.3; however, broadly speaking, such money can be used for the purposes explained to the client.

The definition of client money does not include money received for disbursements which have already been paid, so where money is received in reimbursement of such a payment, it is a receipt of what may conveniently be termed 'business money' by the firm (the term 'business money' will be adopted in this manual). Being business money, it will be paid into a business bank account.

A firm might wish to send a bill to a client for its anticipated future fees and disbursements with a view to paying the money received in payment of that bill into the firm's business bank account and thereby avoid the requirement under Rule 2.1(d) that money received for unbilled fees and disbursements be paid into the client bank account. This is permitted under the Rules, but firms should be cautious about billing for future items (see **2.6.3**).

Example

- *A firm receives £1,000 generally on account of costs.*

  This is client money and must be held in the client bank account. It can be used to make payments on the client's behalf.

- *A firm makes a payment of £100 from its business bank account for a client. The client gives the firm £100 in reimbursement.*

  This is money received for a paid disbursement and must be held in the business bank account.

2.3 Client accounts

A client bank account is one opened by the firm in the name of the firm but used for client money. Rule 3 requires such an account to be at a bank or building society in England and Wales and to include the word 'client' in its title to distinguish it from the firm's own business accounts.

Including the word 'client' in the title has an added significance: s 85(2) of the Solicitors Act 1974 provides that a bank does not have any recourse or right against money in a client bank account in respect of any liability of the solicitor to the bank.

Rule 2.4 requires firms to ensure that client money is available on demand unless an alternative arrangement is agreed in writing with the client or the third party for whom the money is held. This requirement means that firms should not tie up client money in deposit accounts which require extended notice periods.

2.4 Paying money into the client bank account

2.4.1 The general rule

Rule 2.3 provides that client money must be paid promptly into a client bank account. 'Promptly' is not defined or further explained in the Rules. What constitutes 'promptly' will therefore depend on the particular circumstances of the matter and the nature of the firm. However, the requirement to act in the client's best interests and to safeguard client money would suggest the need to act quickly. Indeed, given the widespread availability of internet banking facilities, in many instances the expectation will be that payment must happen immediately.

2.4.2 Exceptions

Rule 2.3 contains the following exceptions to the general rule:

(a) where client money falls within Rule 2.1(c) (money held as a trustee or holder of a specified office or appointment) and paying it into a client bank account would conflict with obligations relating to the specified office or appointment;

(b) the client money represents payments received from the Legal Aid Agency (LAA) for the firm's costs; or

(c) the firm agrees an alternative arrangement in writing with the client, or the third party, for whom the money is held.

The exception in (b) for legal aid payments means that firms can receive these payments into their own business bank accounts. The payment will often include advance payments for parties (such as counsel) providing professional services to the client. There is no requirement for such professionals to be paid within a specified time or for such sums to be transferred to the client bank account if the party providing the professional services is not paid within the specified time.

The lack of such a requirement does not mean that firms will be able to hold payments from the LAA in their business bank account indefinitely. If, for example, a firm does not pay an expert's fee (because the firm retains the money in its account to avoid increasing its overdraft) and thereby delays a client's matter, this would constitute a breach of the rule requiring payments to be made promptly. It is also likely that this would be a breach of the SRA Code of Conduct for Firms, and the firm will almost certainly be in breach of Principle 5 (acting with integrity) and Principle 7 (acting in the client's best interests).

There is a further limited exception to the general rule contained in Rule 2.2. This applies where the only client money received or held falls within Rule 2.1(d) (money for fees and unpaid disbursements received prior to delivery of a bill) and the firm is liable for the disbursement and does not have a client bank account for any other reason. If these conditions are satisfied, the money can be held outside a client bank account, but the firm must inform the client in advance of where and how the money will be held.

An example of an unpaid disbursement for which the firm would be liable is where a firm has an account at the Land Registry and pays monthly for searches or where the firm has instructed counsel on behalf of a client.

The Rule 2.2 exception cannot apply if the firm receives any other types of client money, for example funds to complete the purchase of property or funds held for the beneficiaries of a trust or an estate.

For firms that do fall within the Rule 2.2 exception, there are significant benefits. The ability to dispense with a client bank account results in potential cost savings in areas such as professional indemnity insurance and compliance, as no accountant's report will be required.

2.5 Returning client money

Rule 2.5 requires client money to be returned promptly to the client or the third party for whom the money is held as soon as there is no longer any proper reason to hold those funds.

Again, the Rules do not stipulate any particular time limits, and there is no guidance as to the meaning of promptly. Firms must make their own decisions as to how quickly money should be returned. However, the use of the word 'promptly' signals that the SRA does not expect firms to be dilatory.

A particular issue can arise in relation to aborted transactions. These occur where, for example, a client provides the solicitor with funds for the purchase of a property, but that purchase falls through, and the solicitor is asked to retain the funds whilst the client looks for a new property to buy. In such circumstances, to avoid a breach of Rule 2.5 (and possibly Rule 3.3 - see **2.8**), it will usually be advisable to return the money to the client unless the new transaction is actively being put in place or there are other factors, such as the client history, which would justify the solicitor continuing to hold the funds.

2.6 Keeping client money separate from the firm's own money

Rule 4.1 requires client money to be kept separate from the firm's own money.

2.6.1 Mixed receipts

When, as is often the case, a firm receives a mixed payment containing, for example, client money plus money to pay the firm's bill, Rule 4.2 states that the firm must 'allocate funds promptly' to the correct bank account.

Example

A firm sends a bill for its fees and disbursements to a client, together with a completion statement showing the balance due to complete the client's house purchase. The client sends £300,000 (required to complete the house purchase) plus £360 for the firm's professional charges, plus £1,000 for disbursements the firm has paid.

The money for completion (£300,000) is client money. The money for the fees and billed disbursements (£1,360) is the firm's own money.

Ideally £300,000 should be paid immediately into the client bank account and £1,360 into the firm's own business account. However, this will rarely be practicable. If the client pays by cheque, some banks will allow the cheque to be split between two accounts, but this is unusual. Normally the whole cheque will have to be paid into one account and funds moved promptly to the other account. Similarly, if the client is making an online transfer, the money will usually be paid into one bank account and the firm will need to transfer funds out promptly. The Rules allow the firm to choose whether the money is paid initially into the firm's client or business bank account.

2.6.2 Moving money for fees and disbursements

Firms will normally request money generally on account of costs: the money requested will be intended to cover the firm's fees for its professional services and its future disbursements on behalf of the client. Until a bill is issued, such money is client money and must be paid into the client bank account. Rule 4.3 deals with withdrawing such money and provides:

Where you are holding client money and some or all of that money will be used to pay your costs:

(a) you must give a bill of costs, or other written notification, to the client or the paying party;

(b) this must be done before you transfer any client money from a client account to make the payment; and

(c) any such payment must be for the specific sum identified in the bill of costs or other written notification and covered by the amount held for the particular client or third party.

Where a firm is holding money in the client bank account generally on account of costs and issues a bill, or other written notification of costs, it should transfer the money promptly. However, sometimes, the bill will include an item for a future disbursement which has not yet been paid. For example, in a property transaction, the firm might issue a bill before completion which would include the amount required for stamp duty land tax and Land Registry fees. Moving the money for those items to the business bank account would incur a risk to the client if, for example, the firm became insolvent (see **2.6.3**). SRA guidance, 'Taking money for your firm's costs' (14 September 2020), provides:

> Where the bill does include anticipated disbursements which have not yet been incurred, you will not be considered to be in breach of rule 4.3 by leaving the money associated with those billed anticipated disbursements in the client bank account until such time as they are paid.

2.6.3 Billing for anticipated fees and disbursements

Although the SRA guidance, 'Taking money for your firm's costs' (14 September 2020), accepts that Rule 4.3 permits billing for future work and disbursements and paying the money received into the firm's business account, it highlights the following risks:

- If the client decides to terminate the retainer and asks for the money to be repaid, can the money be paid back immediately?
- If the matter does not proceed, for example the other side pulls out of a transaction, can the money be paid back immediately?
- Following the incapacity or death of a sole practitioner, can the money be paid back immediately?
- If the firm becomes subject to an insolvency event, and the client's money is not held in a ringfenced client account, how will the client be able to progress their matter or pay any disbursements due if they have already paid in advance for these and the insolvency practitioner refuses to repay the client's money because it is held in the firm's business account?

The guidance continues:

> You have an ongoing duty to safeguard money and assets that have been entrusted to you and not prefer your own interests, for example in maintaining cashflow, over those of your clients. The obligation to safeguard money entrusted to you is not limited to only that money which is held in a client account.
>
> You will need to think very carefully about the reasons why you are billing for these sums in advance and the risks to your client in your paying these monies into your firm's business account. It is important to remember that the sending of a bill in these circumstances does not mean that this money is no longer a client's money and it does not need to be safeguarded because it does not sit in a client account.
>
> In all cases, you will therefore need to think carefully about whether your broader obligations properly allow you to bill for such payments and receive money into your business account.
>
> We would not expect firms to bill for advance disbursements that the client will remain liable to pay for such as Stamp Duty Land Tax, and to receive such money into the firm's business account. In our view, this would be improper and a breach of our Standards and Regulations. Until the disbursement is paid the client remains liable for it, and this may be for a significant sum. Therefore, any risk to your firm's business account could result in the transaction failing or the client having to pay twice. Billing to receive money in these circumstances is likely to fail to meet obligations to act in the best interests of your client, safeguard their money or possibly act with integrity.
>
> In all cases where you may be considering billing for such advance payments, you will therefore need to think carefully about whether your broader obligations properly allow you to do this.
>
> If you do consider it is proper, you will need to make sure that your client is fully informed of the risks around their money being received into your firm's business account. How you explain the risks to clients may depend on the nature of your client and any vulnerability they may have.

Knowing these risks, your client might only be prepared to pay a bill sent for work that has been done and disbursements for which you are liable and have been incurred by you.

Reporting Accountants are also likely to qualify a report (see **Chapter 10**) if their view is such that money belonging to the client is, has been or may be placed at risk.

In December 2022 the SRA issued a consultation on minor amendments to the SRA Standards and Regulations. Law firms complained that, despite the SRA's guidance, there was still a lack of clarity as to circumstances in which it is appropriate to transfer money from the client bank account to the business bank account for anticipated costs. Although any amendments were put on hold for a time, the SRA has now confirmed that it intends to make changes to Rule 2.1(d) to make it clear that money for unpaid disbursements remains client money despite the delivery of a bill or other written notification of costs until the disbursement is paid.

2.6.4 Transferring money for paid disbursements

When the current SRA Accounts Rules were first introduced, there was a concern that firms would have to issue a bill, or other written notification of costs, if they wanted to move money from the client bank account to reimburse themselves for disbursements which have already been paid on behalf of the client, for example, where the firm has paid for a Land Registry search or court fee using its own money (often by a direct debit from the firm's business account). The SRA has settled the point in its guidance, 'Taking money for your firm's costs' (20 September 2020).

The guidance states that Rule 5 (see **2.7**) permits money to be withdrawn from the client bank account '*for the purpose for which it is being held*'. Provided the firm has made it clear to the client that the client money in question may be used to reimburse the firm for payments made, this will be permitted without issuing a bill, or other written notification of costs, under Rule 5. The explanation may be made in a client care letter, the firm's terms of engagement or in other communication with the client.

In the SRA Consultation referred to above on 'minor amendments', the SRA proposed to make a change to the wording of Rule 4 to make it clear that withdrawing money for paid disbursements is permissible without a bill. It proposed a new Rule 4.4 to say that the obligation to deliver a bill contained in Rule 4.3 does not apply where 'you withdraw client money from a client account in full or partial reimbursement of money spent by you on behalf of the client, or the third party for whom the money is held'. Although the amendment was put on hold, the SRA has now said that it intends to proceed with the change to Rule 4.

Rule 5 does not permit a transfer where disbursements have not yet been incurred or have not been paid by the firm.

2.7 Withdrawals of client money from the client bank account

2.7.1 Circumstances in which money can be withdrawn

Client money can only be withdrawn in one of the following circumstances (Rule 5.1):

(a) for the purpose for which it is being held; or

(b) following receipt of instructions from the client or the third party for whom the money is held; or

(c) on the SRA's prior written authorisation or in prescribed circumstances.

Rule 5.2 requires all withdrawals to be appropriately authorised and supervised.

Rule 5.3 is particularly important: withdrawals can only be made from the client bank account for a client if sufficient funds are held in the account for that client. If more is taken for one client than is held for them, the balance represents money held for other clients. Using money held for one client for the purpose of another client would constitute a breach of the Rules. Breaches of the Rules and errors must be corrected promptly upon discovery and any money improperly withdrawn must be immediately replaced (Rule 6).

A firm must be careful if it is holding client money generally on account of costs and a disbursement needs to be paid. If the disbursement exceeds the amount of client money held, the firm must not make the payment from the client bank account. Options are as follows:

(a) The payment can be made from the firm's business bank account. Money cannot be transferred from the client bank account to partially reimburse the firm unless a bill is issued or the firm made the client aware that it would be used in this way.

(b) The firm can advance its own money to the client in such cases. This is useful where there is almost enough client money to make the payment. The advance becomes client money and subject to the Rules applying to client money.

2.7.2 Residual client account balances

A residual client account balance is money that the firm has not returned to the client at the end of the retainer and it is now difficult to return the money because, for example, the firm cannot trace the client, or the client has died and the executors are unknown or, occasionally, the client will not accept the money (eg because doing so would affect their entitlement to welfare benefits). Given that Rule 2.5 requires client money to be returned to the client promptly as soon as there is no longer a proper reason to hold the funds, it should rarely be the case that a firm has a residual client account balance.

Rule 5.1 sets out the circumstances in which money can be withdrawn from the client bank account including, under Rule 5.1(c), 'on the SRA's prior written authorisation or in prescribed circumstances'. The SRA has issued a mandatory statement which prescribes the circumstances in which a withdrawal of client money can be made without prior authorisation from the SRA. Those prescribed circumstances are limited to a withdrawal of residual client balances of £500 or less on any one client matter, provided that the money is then paid to charity. The prescribed circumstances also require the firm to have taken reasonable steps to return the money to the client and to keep proper records of what has been done.

For residual client balances over £500, the firm must apply to the SRA for authorisation to make the withdrawal. The SRA has issued separate guidance, 'Granting authority to withdraw residual client balances', setting out the matters it will take into account when considering such applications.

Failure to comply with the Rules is regarded by the SRA as a serious matter as the firm is effectively retaining money which belongs to the client. Anecdotal evidence is that a failure to have policies in place to deal properly with residual client balances is a common reason for accountants to qualify their report on a firm (see **10.2**).

2.8 Improper use of a client bank account as a banking facility

2.8.1 The prohibition

Rule 3.3 provides that the client bank account must not be used to provide banking facilities for clients or third parties. Payments into, and transfers or withdrawals from, a client account must relate to the provision of regulated services.

The point here is that a solicitor should only hold money for the purpose of facilitating legal transactions, not for the client's convenience. Therefore, a solicitor should only receive money and make payments which relate to a legal transaction. However, clients will often ask the solicitor to take other steps on their behalf which have no connection to the transaction, such as using money left following the sale of a property to settle an unrelated debt or to make a transfer of funds to a third party. The solicitor may be lulled into agreeing to the client's request so as to be 'helpful' or in an attempt to avoid upsetting the client by refusing. However, by making such payments, the solicitor is likely to fall foul of Rule 3.3.

Failure to comply with the prohibition is a serious matter. Not only will there be a breach of the Rule itself, the solicitor may also be found to have failed to act in accordance with the fundamental professional and ethical standards set out in the SRA Principles including Principle 1 (upholding the constitutional principle of the rule of law, and the proper administration of justice), Principle 2 (upholding public trust and confidence in the solicitors' profession and in legal services), Principle 3 (independence) and Principle 5 (integrity). A failure to comply with Rule 3.3 is a common reason for accountants to qualify their report on a firm (see **10.2**).

There is an obvious link with money laundering. Money launderers who want to hide the illicit source of their funds will often try to pass money through a legitimate business. It is important for solicitors to be alert to this danger. The SRA considers a breach of anti-money laundering obligations to be a serious matter.

Example

A solicitor has a client who regularly instructs the solicitor to act on his behalf in property transactions. The property transactions always fail to complete. The client gives the solicitor large amounts to cover deposits and expenses which the solicitor pays into the firm's client bank account and periodically returns to client (less professional charges) using a firm cheque. The client never queries the firm's charges.

The solicitor should be suspicious of this pattern of behaviour and report the matter to the firm's money laundering officer.

2.8.2 SRA warning notice

The SRA has issued a warning notice to solicitors about the improper use of client accounts as a banking facility. The notice is intended to help those regulated by the SRA to understand their obligations and how to comply with them. It states:

> Law firms, their managers and employees should not allow the firm's client account to be used to provide banking facilities to clients or third parties. You must also actively consider whether there are any risk factors suggesting that the transaction on which you are acting, even if it appears to be the normal work of a solicitor, is not genuine or is suspicious.

The warning notice explains that providing banking facilities through a client account is objectionable in itself. It says that the prohibition in Rule 3.3, '*You must not use a client account to provide banking facilities to clients or third parties*', is simple and clear. The Rule is not intended to prevent usual practice in traditional work undertaken by solicitors such as conveyancing, company acquisitions, the administration of estates or dealing with formal trusts. It does not prevent firms making usual and proper payments from the client bank account which are related to a transaction (such as the payment of estate agents' fees in a conveyancing transaction).

Whether there is a proper connection will depend on the facts of each case, but simply having a retainer with a client is insufficient to allow for processing funds freely through the client bank account. The question to ask is whether there is any justification for money to pass through the client bank account when it could be paid directly by the client.

Historically, some solicitors held funds for clients to enable them to pay the client's routine outgoings. This was mainly for the clients' convenience such as where they were long-term private clients or based abroad. The SRA warning notice says:

> In view of technological change, such as the ease of internet and telephone banking, we consider that allowing a client account to be used in this way is no longer justifiable and a breach of rule 3.3. Clients can now operate their bank accounts from their own homes or indeed from anywhere in the world. Allowing clients simply to hold money in a client account gives rise to significant risks and may evade sophisticated controls and risk analyses that banks apply to money held for their customers.

It continues:

> Factors you should bear in mind when considering such issues include:
>
> - Throughout the retainer, you should question why you are being asked to receive funds and for what purpose. The further the details of the transaction are from the norm or from the usual legal or professional services a solicitor provides, the higher the risk that you may breach rule 3.3.
> - You should always ask why you are being asked to make a payment or why the client cannot make or receive the payment directly themselves. The client's convenience is not a legitimate reason, nor is not having access to a bank account in the UK. Risk factors could involve the payment of substantial sums to others, including family members, or to corporate entities, particularly overseas, if there is no reason why the client could not receive the money into their own account and transfer it from there.
> - You have a separate obligation to return client money to the client or third party promptly, as soon as there is no longer any proper reason for you to hold those funds (Rule 2.5 of the Accounts Rules). If you retain funds in client account after completion of a transaction, there is risk (depending on how long you hold the money) of breaching both Rules 2.5 and 3.3

Rule 3.3 is to a large extent a preventative provision, intended to make it more difficult for people to use regulated businesses for improper purposes but also to deter law firms from helping such people. Any impropriety may be distant from the movement of money through a client account. In a classic laundering process, the movement through a client account may be the third or fourth stage of laundering the proceeds of a distant crime. But every stage contributes to the effectiveness of the laundering process.

It should also be noted that any exemption or exclusion under the Financial Services and Markets Act 2000 is likely to be lost if a deposit is taken in circumstances which do not form part of regulated services.

Although allowing a client account to be used as a banking facility can facilitate money laundering, Rule 3.3 exists independently of the anti-money laundering legislation and a breach of Rule 3.3 does not require there to be evidence of laundering. There are other dangers such as concealing the ownership of funds during a divorce or avoiding money being caught in an insolvency. There is guidance accompanying the SRA Accounts Rules which contains case studies illustrating such cases.

2.9 Client accounting systems and controls

The client bank account will contain client money held for many different clients, so it is necessary for firms to maintain accurate records, showing for each client:

- all receipts and payments of client money;
- all payments made on behalf of the client from the firm's own money; and
- bills issued to the client.

Rule 8.1(a) requires firms to maintain a client ledger account for each client identified by their name and an appropriate description of the matter. The client ledger account must show all receipts and payments of client money. It must also record any payments made by the firm from its own money on behalf of the client, the issue of bills to the client and any receipts of money in payment of such bills.

Rule 8.1(b) requires firms to maintain a list of all the balances shown by the client ledger accounts of the liabilities to clients (and third parties) with a running total of those balances shown.

Rule 8.1(c) requires firms to have a separate cash book which shows all transactions through client bank accounts. There is no requirement to maintain a cash book to show dealings with the firm's own money, but firms will obviously choose to do so.

Rule 8.2 requires firms to obtain bank statements for all client bank accounts and for the firm's own business bank accounts at least every five weeks, and Rule 8.3 requires the firm to prepare bank reconciliation statements for the client bank accounts. This requires a careful checking of the figures. First, the cash book must be brought up to date to reflect any unexpected items appearing on the bank statement (for example, a dishonoured cheque which has not yet been notified to the firm). Then, the figures on the bank statement must be adjusted to reflect the fact that, for example, when a firm makes a payment using client money this will appear in the firm's accounting records as soon as the cheque is written, but it will not appear on the bank statement until the cheque is presented to the bank for payment. Hence the need to 'reconcile' the bank statement with the firm's records. Any discrepancies revealed by the reconciliation must be investigated promptly.

Carrying out client account reconciliations is important. They often raise the first 'red flag' that something has gone awry in the firm's record keeping, that the Rules have been breached or, perhaps, that there are systematic failures in the firm's policies and procedures. Consequently, failure to comply with the Rules is considered by the SRA to be a serious matter. Failure to carry out client account reconciliations is a common reason for accountants to qualify their report on a firm (see **10.2**).

Rule 8.4 requires a central record of bills and other written notifications of costs to be kept in a readily accessible form.

Firms that do not operate a client account do not need to comply with the record-keeping requirements in Rule 8.1(b) and (c), but they must keep the readily accessible central record of bills or written notifications of costs given as required by Rule 8.4.

On 20 June 2024, the SRA issued a Warning Notice, 'Money missing from client account'. The Warning Notice makes the point that any deficiency on the client account exposes clients and others to a risk of financial loss and damage to public confidence. Missing money must be replaced with extreme urgency even where the shortage has occurred due to circumstances beyond the firm's control (eg theft or cyber-attack). There must be proper systems and controls in compliance with the Accounts Rules, and it is for a firm's principals to ensure that this is the case.

Summary

- A firm must keep client money separate from the firm's own money.
- Subject to exceptions, client money must be paid into a client bank account promptly.
- Firms must never withdraw more client money for a client than is held in the client bank account for that client.
- A client account cannot be used to provide banking facilities.
- All dealings with client money must be recorded.

Sample questions

Question 1

A firm of solicitors receives a number of payments from separate clients over the course of a week.

Which of the following is a receipt of pure client money?

A A cheque for £1,200 in payment of the firm's bill for professional charges.

B A cheque for £50 in reimbursement of an as yet unbilled payment made from the firm's business bank account.

C A cheque for £200 to cover a disbursement as yet unpaid.

D A cheque for £300,600 comprising £300,000 completion money on the client's purchase of a flat and £600 in payment of the firm's bill.

E A cheque for £100 in respect of a disbursement already paid by the firm.

Answer

Option C is correct. Only the cheque for the unpaid disbursement falls within the definition of client money (in Rule 2.1). Options A, B and E are wrong as they all fall outside the definition and therefore represent a receipt of business money. Option D is a mixed receipt: the completion money is client money and the money in payment of the bill is business money.

Question 2

A solicitor is instructed by a client in the purchase of a house. The purchase price agreed with the seller is £400,000. Prior to any disbursements being incurred, the client sends the solicitor a cheque for £40,500 comprising £40,000 to use as the deposit for the purchase and £500 generally on account of costs and disbursements.

Which of the following best describes how the solicitor should deal with receipt of the cheque?

A Split the cheque by paying £500 into the business bank account and £40,000 into the client bank account.

B Pay the entire sum into the business bank account and then transfer £40,000 into the client bank account.

C Pay the entire sum into the business bank account.

D Pay the entire sum into the client bank account.

E Pay the entire sum into the client bank account and then transfer £500 into the business bank account.

Answer

Option D is correct. Money for the deposit and money generally on account of costs and disbursements both fall within the definition of client money. The entire receipt is therefore client money. Client money must be paid promptly into the client bank account (Rule 2.3).

Question 3

A solicitor has acted for a client in respect of commercial property transactions for many years. The solicitor completes the sale of a property on behalf of a client. The proceeds of sale are received into the firm's client bank account. The solicitor is about to transfer the proceeds of sale to the client when the client instructs the solicitor to pay £10,000 from the proceeds of sale to the school attended by the client's son in payment of school fees.

Should the solicitor make the payment?

A Yes, because the solicitor must act in accordance with the client's instructions.

B Yes, because there is no risk of money laundering.

C Yes, because this would comply with the solicitor's duty to act in the client's best interests.

D No, because it is not the purpose for which the money was being held.

E No, because it would be an improper use of the client account as a banking facility.

Answer

Option E is correct. Making the payment would be a breach of Rule 3.3. There is no link between the payment and the legal work carried out by the solicitor. The client could receive the proceeds of sale and then simply make the payment direct. The client's convenience does not justify the improper use of the client account.

3 Common Accounting Entries

SQE1 syllabus

This chapter will help you to achieve the SQE1 Assessment Specification in relation to Functioning Legal Knowledge concerned with the core principles of double entry bookkeeping and the SRA Accounts Rules on:

- payments into and withdrawals from the client account;
- recording bills;
- accounting entries required.

Note that for SQE1, candidates are not usually required to recall specific case names or cite statutory or regulatory authorities.

Learning outcomes

By the end of this chapter you will be able to apply relevant core principles of double entry bookkeeping and the SRA Accounts Rules appropriately and effectively, at the level of a competent newly qualified solicitor in practice, to realistic client-based ethical problems and situations in the following areas:

- Dealing with receipts and payments of client money and the firm's own money.
- Making entries to deal with professional charges and VAT when issuing a bill.

3.1 Introduction

Law firms keep their accounting records in accordance with the core principles of the double entry bookkeeping system. Firms must also comply with the SRA Accounts Rules which are primarily concerned with keeping client money safe and ensuring that proper records are kept. The accounting entries made by law firms must therefore take account of both bookkeeping principles and the Rules.

This chapter looks at:

- the need for law firms to have two sets of accounting records;
- the format of accounts;
- accounting entries for receipts;
- accounting entries for payments;
- recording professional charges.

3.2 The two sets of accounting records

The accounts of most law firms are complicated by the fact that they handle client money which, under Rule 4.1, must be kept separate from the firm's own money. This means that firms need a more sophisticated set of day-to-day accounts than most other businesses. It is essential that all the records of 'client money' dealings are clearly separated from the records of the ordinary business dealings of the firm. Rule 8 sets out the recording requirements of the Rules.

In simple terms law firms can be thought of as carrying on two separate businesses with two separate sets of accounts. This means that the law firm would need one set (Set A) for the first business - say the business which handles client money - and another set (Set B) for the second - say the firm's ordinary business accounts. This explains the reason for one of the fundamental bookkeeping rules for firms providing legal services. The two sets of accounts are entirely separate. Therefore, a firm cannot enter a debit on one set of accounts (Set A) and a credit on the other set (Set B).

3.3 The format of accounts

3.3.1 Requirements as to formats

Law firms may choose any of the various systems on the market which enable the recording requirements of Rule 8 to be satisfied. All such systems are based on the principles of double entry bookkeeping. Guidance issued by the SRA 'Helping you keep accurate client accounting records' includes the following:

- Your books should be maintained on the double-entry principle. This means that every transaction relating to client money should be recorded in at least the client cash book and the client ledger.
- Your books should be legible, up to date and contain narratives alongside the entries which identify and provide adequate information about the transaction. The current balance, if not shown on the client ledger account, should be readily ascertainable. In accordance with Rule 8, entries should be made in chronological order and record the date of the underlying transaction.

- Ledger accounts should include the name of the client or other person or trust for whom the money is held and contain a heading which provides a description of the matter or transaction, for example, Client: Mr A Nother: Matter: sale of 1 Property Road, London. This will help you link the money held or received with those for whom it is held.
- Business account entries (which reflect, for example, money due to your firm for costs) in relation to each client or trust matter are kept up to date as well as the client account entries. This is because it is important to make sure that any credit balances on the business side of the client ledger in respect of client or trust matters are reviewed on a regular basis, for example, at the same time you carry out client account reconciliations, and fully investigated in case of any impact on the client or trust matter and the monies you hold for them.
- You keep a separate contemporaneous and chronological record of any inter-ledger transfers.

3.3.2 The dual cash account

All businesses will need a cash account to record dealings with each bank account. A law firm is required by Rule 8.1(c) to keep a cash account for dealings with the client bank account. The Rules do not require firms to have a cash account to record dealings with its own money, but obviously no business can function without a record of cash received and spent. Therefore, the law firm will need (at least) two separate cash accounts. To ease the administrative burden of actually moving from a cash account in one place to another cash account in a different place and back again, the normal format is to have the two individual cash accounts on the same page next to one another. One set of columns for 'Date' and 'Details' will accommodate both accounts. The Rules use the term 'business' account for the account(s) holding the firm's own money.

Cash account: business

Date	Details	DR	CR	BAL

Cash account: client

Date	Details	DR	CR	BAL

Cash account

Date	Details	Business account			Client account		
		DR	CR	BAL	DR	CR	BAL

3.3.3 The dual ledger account for each client

Rule 8.1 requires dealings with client money on behalf of a client to be recorded. It also requires the issue of bills to a client, payments of the firm's own money on behalf of clients and receipts in payment of bills to be recorded. This requires two separate ledger accounts although, as with the two cash accounts, it is usual to combine the two ledger accounts to show them side by side.

Client ledger account: business

Date	Details	DR	CR	BAL

Client ledger account: client

Date	Details	DR	CR	BAL

Client ledger account

Date	Details	Business account			Client account		
		DR	CR	BAL	DR	CR	BAL

3.4 Receipts of money

In order to make the accounting entries for a receipt of money the first step is to identify whether the receipt is of business money or client money. The receipt can then be recorded in the correct section.

The entry in the cash account for a receipt is a DR entry.

The corresponding CR entry is in the ledger account of the client from whom, or on whose behalf, the money is received.

Receipts of client money will be held for the relevant client in the client bank account.

Receipts of business money will reduce the indebtedness of the relevant client to the firm.

In the examples that follow, the running balances on the cash account are not completed. The amount of the balance depends on the total funds held in the bank at the time. A receipt will increase the balance, and a payment will reduce it. The balance on the cash account is not referable to any one client.

Example

A client, Khan, owes a firm £100 following the issue of a bill. (This means there is a DR balance of £100 on the business columns of Khan's ledger account.) The firm receives £20 from the client to reduce his debt. This is a receipt of business money. It reduces the amount Khan owes the firm.

DR Cash account
CR Khan ledger account } *Business section*

Client: Khan Matter:		Business account			Client account		
Date	**Details**	**DR**	**CR**	**BAL**	**DR**	**CR**	**BAL**
	Balance Cash		 20	100DR 80DR			

Cash account		Business account			Client account		
Date	**Details**	**DR**	**CR**	**BAL**	**DR**	**CR**	**BAL**
	Balance			xxx			xxx
	Khan	20		xxx			

Example

A firm receives £300 from a client, Wiseman, on account of costs. This is a receipt of client money. The firm will hold the money for Wiseman in its client bank account.

DR Cash account } *Client section*
CR Wiseman ledger account

Client: Wiseman Matter:		Business account			Client account		
Date	**Details**	**DR**	**CR**	**BAL**	**DR**	**CR**	**BAL**
	Cash					300	300CR

Cash account		Business account			Client account		
Date	**Details**	**DR**	**CR**	**BAL**	**DR**	**CR**	**BAL**
	Balance						xxx
	Wiseman				300		xxx

3.5 Payments of money

In order to make the accounting entries for a payment of money the first step is to identify whether the payment is to be made from the firm's own business bank account or from its client bank account. The payment can then be recorded in the appropriate cash account.

The entry on the cash account for a payment is a CR entry.

The corresponding double entry is a DR in the ledger account of the client on whose behalf the payment is made.

If the payment is made from the business bank account, the resulting DR balance on the business columns of the client ledger account will show that the client owes the firm money, ie, is a debtor. If the payment is made from the client bank account, it will reduce the amount held for the client (ie it will reduce the CR balance on the client columns of the client ledger account).

Under Rule 5.3 a payment must not be made from a client bank account unless the firm is holding sufficient funds in its client bank account for that client. So, if a firm needs to make a payment for a client but holds no money for that client, the payment must be made from the business bank account.

Example

A firm is holding client money of £500 for a client, Jenkins, generally on account of costs. The firm needs to make a payment of £400 for Jenkins. The firm holds sufficient client money for Jenkins to be able to make the payment using client money.

CR Cash account } *Client section*
DR Jenkins ledger account

Client: Jenkins Matter:		**Business account**			**Client account**		
Date	**Details**	**DR**	**CR**	**BAL**	**DR**	**CR**	**BAL**
	Balance						500CR
	Cash				400		100CR

Cash account		**Business account**			**Client account**		
Date	**Details**	**DR**	**CR**	**BAL**	**DR**	**CR**	**BAL**
	Balance						xxx
	Jenkins					400	xxx

3.6 Recording the firm's professional charges

When the firm issues a bill to the client, it will include an item for its professional charges and VAT on those charges. The solicitor will want to make entries in the accounts to show that the client owes the firm the charges and VAT.

At this stage, there is no movement of cash, so no entry is made in the cash account.

On the client ledger account, there must be recorded DR entries for professional charges and VAT. The entries must be made in the business section. This is because the purpose of the DR entries is to show that the client owes money to the firm.

The corresponding CR entries are made on an income ledger account and an account in the name of His Majesty's Revenue and Customs (HMRC) respectively.

The income ledger account could be called 'professional charges' or 'professional fees'. Traditionally it has been called 'profit costs'.

At the end of the year, the balance on the profit costs account will show the amount the firm has billed for professional charges. The HMRC ledger account shows how much the firm owes HMRC in VAT.

Example

A firm issues a bill for £400 profit costs plus £80 VAT to a client, Hale.

DR Hale ledger account £400 } *Business section*

DR Hale ledger account £80

CR Profit costs account £400

CR HMRC account £80

Client: Hale **Matter:**		**Business account**			**Client account**		
Date	**Details**	**DR**	**CR**	**BAL**	**DR**	**CR**	**BAL**
	Profit costs VAT	400 80		400DR 480DR			

Profit Costs

Date	**Details**	**DR**	**CR**	**BAL**
	Hale		400	400CR

HMRC

Date	**Details**	**DR**	**CR**	**BAL**
	Hale		80	80CR

When a firm sends a bill, it will include details of disbursements already paid on the client's behalf and, where appropriate, disbursements to be paid in the future. As clients will normally have provided money on account of costs, it is usual to provide an accompanying statement setting out how much of the client's money has been used already, and whether further funds are required from the client to meet the firm's professional charges and future disbursements or whether there is a balance to be returned to the client.

No entries are made on the accounts in relation to disbursements when the bill is sent. Disbursements are recorded as and when they are paid.

When a bill has been issued for professional charges and paid and/or unpaid disbursements, money received in payment of the bill will be the firm's own money and must be paid into the business bank account.

Summary

- A law firm will have two cash accounts: one for business money and one for client money. They are frequently shown side by side.
- A law firm will have two client ledger accounts: one for business money dealings and one for client money dealings. They are frequently shown side by side.
- When dealing with cash receipts or payments, the first step is to identify whether it involves business money or client money, then the receipt or payment can be recorded in the appropriate section of the accounts.
- The entries for a receipt are:
    - CR on client ledger account;
    - DR on cash account; and
    - in the business or client section as appropriate.
- The entries for a payment are:
    - DR on client ledger account;
    - CR on cash account; and
    - in the business or client section as appropriate.
- When a bill is sent, entries are made:
    - to record professional charges with a DR entry in the business section of the client ledger account and a CR entry in the profit costs account; and
    - to record VAT with a DR entry in the business section of the client ledger account and a CR entry in the HMRC account.
- No entries are made in relation to disbursements when a bill is sent. Disbursements are recorded when they are paid.

Sample questions

Question 1

A solicitor receives £1,000 from a client generally on account of costs. Following the receipt, the client ledger account shows a CR balance of £1,000 on the client section and a zero balance on the business section. The solicitor needs to pay a court fee of £300 on the client's behalf. The solicitor makes the payment from the firm's client bank account and records the payment accordingly in the firm's accounts. The solicitor has not issued a bill.

Which of the following best describes the effect of the payment?

A The client owes the firm £300.

B There is a DR balance of £300 on the business section of the client ledger account.

C The firm is holding £700 on the client's behalf.

D There is a CR balance of £300 on the client section of the client ledger account.

E The solicitor is in breach of the SRA Accounts Rules.

Answer

Option C is correct. The firm was holding sufficient money in the client bank account on behalf of the client to make the payment. Using client money to make the payment was not a breach of the Rules. Once the payment has been made, the CR balance on the client section of the client ledger account reduces to £700. This shows that the firm is now holding £700 on behalf of the client.

Question 2

A firm sends a bill for professional charges to a client. The firm receives a cheque from the client in payment of the bill.

Which of the following pair of double entries shows how the receipt of the cheque should be recorded?

A CR cash account business section.
DR profit costs account business section.

B CR client ledger account business section.
DR cash account business section.

C CR profit costs account business section.
DR client ledger account business section.

D CR client ledger account client section.
DR cash account client section.

E CR profit costs account client section.
DR client ledger account client section.

Answer

Option B is correct. Money received in payment of a bill is the firm's own money and must be paid into the business bank account. It must therefore be recorded in the business section of the appropriate accounts (meaning that options D and E are wrong). The firm has received money. The entries for a receipt are CR on the client ledger account and DR on the cash account. Options A and C are wrong as no entries are necessary on the profit costs account when a bill is paid.

4 Transfers and Mixed Receipts

SQE1 syllabus

This chapter will help you to achieve the SQE1 Assessment Specification in relation to Functioning Legal Knowledge concerned with the core principles of double entry bookkeeping and the SRA Accounts Rules on:

- keeping and maintaining accurate records;
- transfers;
- requirement to pay client money into a client account;
- accounting entries required.

Note that for SQE1, candidates are not usually required to recall specific case names or cite statutory or regulatory authorities.

Learning outcomes

By the end of this chapter you will be able to apply relevant core principles of double entry bookkeeping and the SRA Accounts Rules appropriately and effectively, at the level of a competent newly qualified solicitor in practice, to realistic client-based ethical problems and situations in the following areas.

- The distinction between cash transfers and inter-client transfers;
- The accounting entries required to record transfers;
- Dealing with receipts that are a mixture of business and client money.

4.1 Introduction

Rule 8.1(a) requires firms to record on each client's ledger account all client and business money receipts and payments made for that client on the client and business section of the accounts, as appropriate. Therefore, if a client's money is withdrawn from the client bank account and paid into the business bank account, for example to pay the firm's charges, this must be recorded. This type of transfer is called a cash transfer.

A firm must keep a running total of the amount owed to each client, so if a firm is holding money in the client bank account for one client and stops holding the money to the order of the first client and starts holding it to the order of a second client, the change in ownership of the money must be recorded. This type of transfer is called an inter-client transfer.

A firm will often receive funds from clients that are a mixture of business money and client money. Rule 4.2 requires such funds to be allocated promptly to the correct bank account.

This chapter looks at:

- cash transfers;
- inter-client transfers;
- mixed receipts.

4.2 Cash transfers

The most common situation in which a cash transfer will occur is where money is withdrawn from the client bank account and paid into the business bank account to pay the firm's professional charges. Once a bill (or other written notification) has been issued, a firm can transfer money from the client bank account to the business bank account for its own professional fees, including any VAT element, and, where relevant, any disbursements included on the bill.

Other reasons for cash transfers include:

(a) to advance money to a client or trust where the solicitor needs to make a payment on behalf of the client or trust and insufficient client money is available (once advanced, the money becomes client money);

(b) to replace money withdrawn in breach of Rule 5.3; and

(c) to allow the client a sum in lieu of interest.

Recording a transfer from the client bank account to the business bank account is done in two stages:

(1) Record the payment of money from the client bank account:

CR Cash account DR Client's ledger account	} Client section

(2) Record the receipt of money into the business bank account:

DR Cash account CR Client's ledger account	} Business section

Example

On 10 April, a firm receives £800 from its client, Andoh, on account of costs to be incurred.

The £800 is client money. It will be paid into the client bank account and recorded in Andoh's ledger account and in the cash account.

Client: Andoh Matter: Miscellaneous		**Business account**			**Client account**		
Date	**Details**	**DR**	**CR**	**BAL**	**DR**	**CR**	**BAL**
April 10	Cash. From Andoh. On account					800	800CR

Cash account		**Business account**			**Client account**		
Date	**Details**	**DR**	**CR**	**BAL**	**DR**	**CR**	**BAL**
April 10	Andoh				800		xxx

On 26 April, the firm sends Andoh a bill for £400 plus £80 VAT.

When the bill is issued, the entries for profit costs and VAT will be DR entries on Andoh's ledger account (entries for profit costs and VAT on the issue of a bill are debited in the business section to show that the client owes the firm money).

The CR entries will be on the profit costs and HMRC account which are not shown.

Client: Andoh Matter: Miscellaneous		**Business account**			**Client account**		
Date	**Details**	**DR**	**CR**	**BAL**	**DR**	**CR**	**BAL**
April 10	Cash. From Andoh. On account					800	800CR
26	Profit costs	400		400DR			
	VAT	80		480DR			

Cash account		**Business account**			**Client account**		
Date	**Details**	**DR**	**CR**	**BAL**	**DR**	**CR**	**BAL**
April 10	Andoh				800		xxx

On 28 April, the firm transfers £480 from the client bank account to the business bank account.

(1) To record the payment from the client bank account:

CR Cash account
DR Andoh's ledger account } *Client section*

Client: Andoh **Matter: Miscellaneous**		**Business account**			**Client account**		
Date	**Details**	**DR**	**CR**	**BAL**	**DR**	**CR**	**BAL**
April							
10	Cash. From Andoh. On account					800	800CR
26	Profit costs	400		400DR			
	VAT	80		480DR			
28	Cash. Transfer from client account				480		320CR

Cash account		**Business account**			**Client account**		
Date	**Details**	**DR**	**CR**	**BAL**	**DR**	**CR**	**BAL**
April							
10	Andoh				800		xxx
28	Andoh					480	xxx

(2) To record the receipt of money into the business bank account:

DR Cash account
CR Andoh's ledger account } *Business section*

Client: Andoh **Matter: Miscellaneous**		**Business account**			**Client account**		
Date	**Details**	**DR**	**CR**	**BAL**	**DR**	**CR**	**BAL**
April							
10	Cash. From Andoh. On account					800	800CR
26	Profit costs	400		400DR			
	VAT	80		480DR			
28	Cash. Transfer from client account				480		320CR
	Cash. Transfer to business account		480	—			

Cash account		Business account			Client account		
Date	**Details**	**DR**	**CR**	**BAL**	**DR**	**CR**	**BAL**
April							
10	Andoh				800		xxx
28	Andoh					480	xxx
	Andoh	480					

For the sake of convenience, the payment from the client bank account and the receipt into the business bank account are often shown on the same line:

Client: Andoh Matter: Miscellaneous		Business account			Client account		
Date	**Details**	**DR**	**CR**	**BAL**	**DR**	**CR**	**BAL**
April							
10	Cash. From Andoh. On account					800	800CR
26	Profit costs	400		400DR			
	VAT	80		480DR			
28	Cash. Transfer from client account to business account		480	—	480		320CR

Cash account		Business account			Client account		
Date	**Details**	**DR**	**CR**	**BAL**	**DR**	**CR**	**BAL**
April							
10	Andoh				800		xxx
28	Andoh. Transfer from client account to business account	480				480	xxx

When dealing with bills, there are some important points to keep in mind:

- When a bill has been issued for professional charges and paid and/or unpaid disbursements, money received in payment of the bill will be the firm's own money and must be paid into the business bank account.
- Where the firm is holding client money in the client bank account and issues a bill for professional charges and paid and/or unpaid disbursements, the whole amount billed can be transferred to the business bank account.

- Where the firm is holding client money in the client bank account, money due to the firm for disbursements paid with the firm's own money cannot be transferred unless a bill has been issued or the firm made clear when the money was received that it would be used in this way.
- Even if a bill (or other written notification) has not been issued, money received for a paid disbursement is the firm's own money, not client money.

Note also that billing for unpaid disbursements can cause risks to client money (see **2.6.3**).

4.3 Inter-client transfers

It is sometimes the case that a firm which is holding money in the client bank account for Client A stops holding that money for Client A and starts holding it for Client B. An example would be where A owes B money and asks the firm to hold the money for B. No money is taken out of the client bank account. However, the firm must make changes to the firm's internal accounts to record the change as for whom the money is held. This is necessary to comply with the obligation to show receipts and payments made for each client (Rule 8). This type of transfer is referred to as an 'inter-client' transfer or a 'paper' transfer.

To record an inter-client transfer no entries are made on the cash account as no money is moving in or out of a bank account. Instead a DR entry is made in the client section of the ledger account of the client for whom the money was originally held, and a CR entry is made in the client section of the ledger account of the client for whom the money is now held:

DR Client ledger account of first client

CR Client ledger account of second client

Example

A solicitor is instructed by a client, Anne Brown, to collect a debt of £10,000 from White & Co. The solicitor writes to White & Co requesting payment. On 7 August, the solicitor receives a cheque from White & Co for £10,000 in payment of the debt.

When the £10,000 is received, it is client money held to the order of Anne:

Cash account		**Business account**			**Client account**		
Date	**Details**	**DR**	**CR**	**BAL**	**DR**	**CR**	**BAL**
Aug 7	Anne Brown				10,000		xxx

Client: Anne Brown **Matter: Debt collection**		**Business account**			**Client account**		
Date	**Details**	**DR**	**CR**	**BAL**	**DR**	**CR**	**BAL**
Aug 7	Cash. From White & Co. Debt					10,000	10,000CR

The solicitor also acts for Anne's sister, Jane Brown, who is about to exchange contracts on the purchase of a flat. On 9 August, Anne tells the solicitor that she wants Jane to have £1,000 to put towards the deposit due on exchange and asks the solicitor to hold £1,000 of her money to the order of Jane.

When Anne instructs the solicitor to hold £1,000 to the order of Jane there will be no entry on the cash account. There will be entries on the client ledger accounts of Anne and Jane to show the inter-client transfer:

Client: Anne Brown **Matter: Debt collection**		**Business account**			**Client account**		
Date	**Details**	**DR**	**CR**	**BAL**	**DR**	**CR**	**BAL**
Aug 7	Cash. From White & Co. Debt					10,000	10,000CR
9	Jane Brown. Transfer				1,000		9,000CR

Client: Jane Brown **Matter: Property Purchase**		**Business account**			**Client account**		
Date	**Details**	**DR**	**CR**	**BAL**	**DR**	**CR**	**BAL**
Aug 9	Anne Brown. Transfer					1,000	1,000CR

4.4 Mixed receipts

A law firm will often receive funds from clients that are a mixture of business and client money. Rule 4.2 requires the funds to be allocated promptly to the correct bank account.

Example

A firm pays £40 out of its business bank account on behalf of a client, Carollo Ltd, on 1 February. In response to a request by the firm, the client sends a cheque for £100 on 10 February, partly to pay back the £40 and partly on account of costs. The £40 is business money because it is received for a paid disbursement and the £60 is client money.

4.4.1 Split cheques

If the bank allows it, the firm can 'split' the cheque. This means paying the different parts of the cheque into different bank accounts. Therefore £40 would be paid into the business bank account and the £60 into the client bank account:

DR Business portion to Cash account	-	Business section
DR Client portion to Cash account	-	Client section
CR Business portion to Client ledger account	-	Business section
CR Client portion to Client ledger account	-	Client section

Client: Carollo Ltd **Matter:**		**Business account**			**Client account**		
Date	**Details**	**DR**	**CR**	**BAL**	**DR**	**CR**	**BAL**
Feb							
1	Cash	40		40DR			
10	Cash		40	—		60	60CR

Cash account		**Business account**			**Client account**		
Date	**Details**	**DR**	**CR**	**BAL**	**DR**	**CR**	**BAL**
Feb							
1	Carollo		40				xxx
10	Carollo	40			60		

4.4.2 Direct transfers

Banks are usually unwilling to split cheques in practice as it creates administrative problems for them, so paying the money into one bank account and transferring money is more common. Rule 4.2 provides that money received as a mixed payment must be allocated 'promptly' to the correct account. When a cheque is received which is a mixed receipt the firm can choose whether to pay it initially into the client or business bank account. Firms will have different policies. Some may adopt a fixed rule that all mixed receipts are paid initially into the client bank account. Others may have a more flexible policy, allocating a mixed receipt in accordance with the make-up of the mixed receipt. For example, a firm operating a flexible policy would pay a receipt which is 90% client money, 10% business money into the client bank account but would pay a receipt that was 10% client money, 90% business money into the business bank account.

Rather than paying by cheque, most clients will pay by bank transfer. It is cumbersome to give clients details of both the client bank account and the business bank account. Firms are most likely to give clients details of the client bank account and transfer business money to a business bank account:

DR whole amount to Cash account
CR whole amount to Client ledger account
} Client section

When later transferring business portion:

CR Cash account DR Client ledger account	} Client section
DR Cash account CR Client ledger account	} Business section

Client: Carollo Ltd Matter:		Business account			Client account		
Date	**Details**	**DR**	**CR**	**BAL**	**DR**	**CR**	**BAL**
Feb							
1	Cash	40		40DR			
10	Cash					100	100CR
	Cash transfer		40	—	40		60CR

Cash account		Business account			Client account		
Date	**Details**	**DR**	**CR**	**BAL**	**DR**	**CR**	**BAL**
Feb							
1	Carollo		40				xxx
10	Carollo				100		
	Carollo transfer	40		—		40	

Summary

- Cash transfers from one bank account to another involve a cash payment from one bank account and a cash receipt into the other. One pair of entries records the payment; one pair of entries records the receipt.
- Inter-client transfers do not involve the movement of cash. The cash remains in the client bank account. To record an inter-client transfer there is a DR entry in the client section of the transferor's ledger account and a CR entry in the client section of the transferee's ledger account.
- Money received from a client which is a mixture of business and client money must either be split between the business and client bank account or paid into either the client or business bank account.
- If a mixed receipt is all paid into the client bank account, the business money must be transferred to the business bank account promptly. If it is all paid into the business account, the client money must be transferred to the client bank account promptly.

Sample questions

Question 1

A firm is acting for the executors in the administration of an estate. The firm is holding £300,000 in the client bank account for the executors and sends the estate accounts to the residuary beneficiary for approval. The residuary beneficiary approves the estate accounts and asks the firm to hold £220,000 briefly for her and to hold £80,000 for her son, who is buying a house. The firm is acting for the son in his house purchase and completion is imminent.

Which of the following best describes how the firm should record the residuary beneficiary's instructions in the accounts?

A An inter-client transfer of £80,000 from the executors' ledger account to the son's ledger account.

B An inter-client transfer of £300,000 from the executors' ledger account to a client ledger in the residuary beneficiary's name followed by a cash transfer of £80,000.

C An inter-client transfer of £80,000 from the executors' ledger account to the son's ledger account and an inter-client transfer of £220,000 from the executors' ledger account to a client ledger in the residuary beneficiary's name.

D Two cash transfers: one of £80,000 and one of £220,000.

E An inter-client transfer of £300,000 from the executors' ledger account to a client ledger in the residuary beneficiary's name followed by an inter-client transfer of £80,000 from residuary beneficiary's ledger account to the son's ledger account.

Answer

Option E is correct. Although no money will actually move in or out of the client bank account, ledger entries must accurately reflect for whom money is held in the bank client account. An inter-client transfer must first of all be made to the beneficiary. On approval of the estate accounts the money is held for the residuary beneficiary. It is the beneficiary who instructs the firm to then hold some money on behalf of another person. So, two inter-client transfers must be made.

Question 2

A firm acts for a client in the purchase of a property. The firm sends a bill to the client made up of:

- £480 for the firm's professional charges and VAT
- £600 for a surveyor's fee

The client sends the firm a cheque for £101,080, comprised of £1,080 in payment of the bill and £100,000 as the balance of the purchase price required to complete the purchase.

Which of the following best describes how the firm should deal with receipt of the cheque?

A The firm should split the cheque by paying £480 to the client bank account and £100,600 to the business bank account.

B The firm should pay the whole amount into the client bank account and then make a cash transfer of £600 into the business bank account.

C The firm should pay the whole amount into the business bank account and then make an inter-client transfer of £100,000.

D The firm should pay the whole amount into the business bank account and then make a cash transfer of £100,000 into the client bank account.

E The firm should pay the whole amount into the business bank account and then make a cash transfer of £1,080 into the client bank account.

Answer

Option D is correct. This is a mixed receipt and the funds must be allocated to the correct account promptly. This can be achieved by splitting the cheque correctly, or by paying the whole amount into either the client or business bank account and then making a cash transfer of the correct amount. As a bill has been delivered, the money for professional charges and the surveyor's fee (a total of £1,080) is not client money. The £100,000 for the balance of the purchase price is client money. Therefore, the firm should pay the whole amount into the business bank account and then make a cash transfer of the £100,000 client money into the client bank account (as an alternative, the firm could pay the whole amount into the client bank account and then make a cash transfer of £1,080 into the business bank account).

5 Value Added Tax

SQE1 syllabus

This chapter will enable you to achieve the SQE1 Assessment Specification in relation to Functioning Legal Knowledge concerned with the core principles of double entry bookkeeping and the SRA Accounts Rules on:

- requirement to keep and maintain accurate records;
- the VAT element of the submission and payment of bills;
- disbursements using the agency and principal methods;
- accounting entries required.

Note that for SQE1, candidates are not usually required to recall specific case names or cite statutory or regulatory authorities. Cases are provided for illustrative purposes only.

Learning outcomes

By the end of this chapter you will be able to apply relevant core principles of double entry bookkeeping and the SRA Accounts Rules appropriately and effectively, at the level of a competent newly qualified solicitor in practice, to realistic client-based ethical problems and situations in the following areas:

- The general principles of value added tax;
- The application of value added tax to professional charges and disbursements.

5.1 Introduction

Firms providing legal services are affected by value added tax (VAT). VAT is relevant both to the firm's professional charges and to some disbursements paid by the firm on behalf of clients.

This chapter looks at:

- general principles of VAT; and
- VAT and firms providing legal service.

5.2 General principles

VAT involves two distinct aspects: output tax (charged by a business to its customers) and input tax (charged to the business by its suppliers). A business registered for VAT charges its customers output tax for which it must then account to HMRC. In effect, the business collects the tax for HMRC.

It will normally be possible for such a business to deduct input tax charged to the business from the amount accounted for to HMRC.

The standard rate of VAT is currently 20%. There is also a zero rate (applicable, for example, to food, books and transport) and a reduced rate of 5% (applicable, for example, to domestic fuel and child car seats). Some goods and services, such as insurance and health services, are exempt from VAT.

5.2.1 Output tax

VAT is chargeable on the supply of goods or services where the supply is a taxable supply and is made by a taxable person in the course or furtherance of a business carried on by the taxable person (Value Added Tax Act (VATA) 1994, s 4(1)).

The person making the supply is liable to account to HMRC for the amount of tax which is charged.

5.2.1.1 Supply of goods

This comprises all forms of supply whereby the whole property in goods is transferred, including a gift of goods.

5.2.1.2 Supply of services

This covers anything which is not a supply of goods, but is done for a consideration.
A gratuitous supply of services is not a supply for VAT purposes, in contrast to a gift of goods.

5.2.1.3 Taxable supply

A taxable supply is any supply of goods or services other than an exempt supply.

A firm supplying legal services will be making a standard-rated supply. Legal services include professional charges and some payments made for clients. A solicitor supplying insurance will be making an exempt supply.

5.2.1.4 Taxable person

A person is a taxable person if they are or are required to be registered under VATA 1994. A person must register if, broadly, the value of taxable supplies (not profit) in the preceding 12 months exceeded a figure specified in each year's Budget (currently £90,000). A firm of solicitors will virtually always have to be registered.

Voluntary registration is also permitted. A person may register voluntarily in order to recover input tax charged to them.

5.2.1.5 Business

VAT is chargeable by a taxable person only on taxable supplies made in the course or furtherance of a business carried on by the taxable person.

A firm supplying legal services which is a taxable person must charge VAT not only on its supplies of legal services but also on any other supplies it makes in the course of its business, eg, the sale of redundant office equipment.

5.2.2 Input tax

Where a taxable person is charged VAT on the supply of goods or services for the purposes of their business, they may deduct the tax charged to them from the amount of output tax which they account for to HMRC (s 25(2)). Since input tax charged to a taxable person is recoverable, it follows that VAT is not an expense of a person who makes only taxable supplies, whether at the standard or zero rate.

5.2.3 Value of supply

Where a supply is fully taxable, VAT at the standard rate (20%) is payable on the value of the supply. If the consideration is in money, the value of the supply is such amount as, with the addition of the total tax payable, is equal to the consideration (s 19(2)).

If a price or fee is agreed, this will be deemed to include VAT unless expressly stated to be tax exclusive.

It is important to remember to quote for a fee plus VAT. If VAT is not stated to be extra, the customer will only pay the fee quoted; the business will have to pay the VAT from the quoted fee and will end up with less money than it expected.

5.2.4 Time of supply

The importance of the time of supply (or tax point) is that it decides the quarter at the end of which a taxable person becomes liable to account for output tax on a particular supply. It also determines the quarter in which a taxable person can claim input tax on a taxable supply made to them. The basic tax points are:

(a) Goods: when the goods are removed or made available to the purchaser (s 6(2)).

(b) Services: when the services are completed (s 6(3)).

5.2.5 Tax invoices

Tax invoices are of vital importance to a taxable person since they are evidence of their right to recover the input tax on a supply made to them, ie without such an invoice they will generally be unable to claim an input credit, irrespective of whether or not they have made payment to the supplier.

A taxable person making a taxable supply to another taxable person must, within 30 days after the time of supply (or within such longer period as HMRC allows), provide them with a tax invoice, which includes certain prescribed information.

5.2.6 Collection and accounts

Accounting for VAT will generally be by reference to quarterly accounting periods. Within one month after the end of each quarter, a taxable person must submit a completed return form to HMRC, together with a remittance for the tax due.

Example

During an accounting period, a firm providing legal services sends bills charging total professional charges of £200,000 plus output tax of £40,000. In the same period, the firm buys office equipment for £40,000 plus input tax of £8,000.

The firm accounts to HMRC as follows:

	£
Output tax charged	*40,000*
less input tax suffered	*(8,000)*
Payable to HMRC	*32,000*

The firm has to account for the £32,000 due irrespective of whether or not the customers have yet paid the firm the cash. This can sometimes cause a cashflow problem.

5.3 VAT and firms providing legal services

5.3.1 Professional charges

Firms providing legal services must charge VAT on their supply of services.

Example

Bill	£
Professional charges	*200.00*
VAT @ 20%	*40.00*
Total	*240.00*

The firm will need a ledger account in the name of HMRC as well as a profit costs account and a ledger account in the name of the client.

CR Profit costs account with professional charges

CR HMRC with VAT

DR Client ledger account (business section) with professional charges and VAT as two separate figures

Client: Matter:		Business account			Client account		
Date	**Details**	**DR**	**CR**	**BAL**	**DR**	**CR**	**BAL**
	Profit costs VAT	200 40		200DR 240DR			

Profit costs account

Date	Details	DR	CR	BAL
	Client		200	xxx

HMRC account

Date	Details	DR	CR	BAL
	Client		40	xxx

5.3.2 Disbursements for VAT purposes

As a matter of convenience for the client, firms providing legal services frequently pay expenses (eg court fees) on behalf of the client. Such expenses are often referred to as 'disbursements'. HMRC does not regard 'disbursements' as part of the supply of legal services and so the firm does not have to charge VAT on them. However, to qualify as a disbursement for this purpose, an item must fulfil certain conditions.

HMRC's view of what constitutes a disbursement is set out in para 25.1.1 of HMRC VAT Notice 700. The crucial point is that if these costs are incurred by suppliers in making their own supply to their clients, then they must be included in the value of those supplies when VAT is calculated. If the payment to third parties is made purely as agent for the client then it is a disbursement for VAT purposes, and is not included in the amount on which VAT is charged.

Generally, it is only advantageous to treat a payment as a disbursement (as opposed to part of the supply of legal services) where no VAT is chargeable on the supply by a third party or where the client is not entitled to reclaim it as input tax.

To be a disbursement, the Notice says that all the following conditions must be met:

- you acted as the agent of your client when you paid the third party;
- your client actually received and used the goods or services provided by the third party (this condition usually prevents the agent's own travelling and subsistence expenses, telephone bills, postage, and other costs being treated as disbursements for VAT purposes);
- your client was responsible for paying the third party (examples include estate duty and stamp duty payable by your client on a contract to be made by the client);

- your client authorised you to make the payment on their behalf;
- your client knew that the goods or services you paid for would be provided by a third party;
- your outlay will be separately itemised when you invoice your client; you recover only the exact amount which you paid to the third party; and
- the goods or services, which you paid for, are clearly additional to the supplies which you make to your client on your own account.'

HMRC's view is that all the conditions set out above must be satisfied before a payment can be treated as a disbursement for VAT purposes. The House of Lords decision in *Nell Gwynn House Maintenance Fund Trustees v C&E Commissioners* [1999] STC 79 confirmed that VAT law draws a clear distinction in principle between:

(i) expenses paid to a third party that have been incurred by you in the course of making your own supply of services to your client and which are part of the whole of the services rendered by you to your client; and

(ii) expenses for specific services that have been supplied by the third party to your client and you have merely acted as your client's known and authorised representative in paying the third party.

Only in case (ii) can the amounts of the payments to the third party qualify for treatment as disbursements for VAT purposes.

Examples of disbursements are items where the client is responsible for paying the third party, such as:

- inheritance tax;
- capital gains tax;
- stamp duty and stamp duty land tax;
- estate agents' fees.

Counsel's fees are disbursements as the service is supplied to the client (even though the solicitor is responsible for ensuring payment). The Law Society's Practice Note, 'VAT treatment of disbursements and expenses', says that Land Registry fees for registration of title are disbursements (the position of searches and official copies is different - see below). HMRC's VAT Manual says at VTAXPER46000 that the following can be treated as disbursements:

- statutory charges such as court fees, estate duty, incorporation fees, land charge and land registry fees, probate fees, stamp duty;
- charges for the professional services of a third party. For example, the sale of a property is usually organised by a solicitor, who will present a bill to the vendor for both the solicitor's own services and the commission payable to the estate agent. The supply of the estate agent's services is to the vendor, not the solicitor, and so the solicitor may treat this as a disbursement for VAT purposes. The fees of notaries, surveyors, or witnesses, and charges for police and medical reports may also fall into this category.

The paragraph says that telegraphic transfer fees or CHAPS which represent a charge by the bank to the solicitor for the service of transferring money out of the solicitor's bank account cannot be treated as a disbursement and nor can general expenses borne by the solicitor including travel, accommodation and telephone charges.

Items which do not qualify as disbursements are those which are a necessary part of the service supplied to the client, for example, telephone charges, postage and photocopying charges; these are overheads of the business, and HMRC requires the firm to charge VAT on them. The SRA considers that it is not normally appropriate to make a separate charge for such items, although there may be exceptional cases where it is permissible, eg when unusual amounts of photocopying are involved. Firms normally increase their professional charges to cover these items.

Travelling expenses incurred by a solicitor are not disbursements and must be included as part of the overall charge. This view was upheld in the case of *Rowe & Maw (A Firm) v Customs and Excise Commissioners* [1975] 1 WLR 1291. The court held that the cost of fares incurred by a solicitor in the course of their duties to the client was incurred for the solicitor, not for the client.

Any expenses incurred by a firm in order for it to complete its supply of professional services will not be a disbursement.

There has been some uncertainty as to whether or not search fees could be treated as disbursements. Now HMRC's view, as set out in full in its internal manual 'VAT Taxable Person Manual' (VTAXPER47000), is that whether a fee for a search is to be treated as a disbursement will depend on how the information obtained in the search is used. If it is passed on to the client without comment or analysis, the fee may be treated as a disbursement – it would be relatively unusual for this to be the case. More commonly, the firm will use the information to provide advice or a report and here the fee for the search will form part of the charges for its services and will be subject to VAT.

HMRC said in Revenue and Customs Brief 6 (2020) that revised guidance on VAT disbursements would be published '*to ensure consistency and provide clarity*'. Further guidance is required as there is a lack of clarity in the case law as to what can and cannot be regarded as a disbursement. The Court of Appeal recently indicated that it thought there was a strong case for a position that disbursement treatment should not be available where a solicitor acts as 'more than a postbox'.

The same item may amount to a disbursement in one situation and not in another. For example, a solicitor dealing with the administration of an estate might pay a valuer's fee on a particular asset. This would be a disbursement if the personal representative, who was also a beneficiary and entitled to the asset to be valued, had requested the valuation to assist in the decision as to whether or not to sell the asset, but would not be if the solicitor had requested it in order to calculate the inheritance tax payable on the estate.

The Law Society Practice Note, 'VAT treatment of disbursements and expenses', says that fees for Official Copy entries obtained on the sale of a property are unlikely to fulfil the criteria for a disbursement. The official copies are likely to have been used to provide advice, meaning that the supply of information is a supply to the firm and therefore that the cost must be treated as part of the firm's overall legal services.

5.3.3 The treatment of 'non-disbursements' in the firm's accounts

'Non-disbursements' are payments made to third parties by the firm which do not fall within the narrow definition of disbursements. HMRC sometimes refers to them as 'recharges'. Firms have to treat these items as part of their chargeable supply. It is important the firms do not mis-classify these items as disbursements. If they fail to charge VAT on these items, they are understating their VAT. They will become liable for the underpayment of VAT with interest and penalties.

Firms do not usually make a separate charge for items such as postage, fares and telephone which are really just overheads of the business. They simply make sure that the amount they charge for professional fees is sufficient to cover the overheads.

Search fees could be dealt with similarly by recording the payment using a searches account:

CR Cash account – Business section with the amount paid

If the search fee bears VAT (as most do) the VAT exclusive amount and the VAT will be entered as separate items

DR Searches account

Plus, if the search is taxable

DR HMRC account with the VAT charged to the firm

However, firms will normally want a record of searches incurred for each client so that they are shown separately from professional charges on the bill. It will therefore be necessary to enter on the client ledger account so that they will not be overlooked when a bill is sent. The easiest course is to debit them to the client ledger when they are paid and include a note in the details column that they are part of the firm's taxable supply.

CR Cash account - Business section

If the search fee bears VAT (as most do) the VAT exclusive amount and the VAT will be entered as separate items.

DR Client ledger account business section with the VAT exclusive amount and make a note in the details column that the payment is part of the firm's taxable supply

And, if the search fee is taxable

DR HMRC account with the VAT input tax charged to the firm

When the bill is issued, VAT output tax will be charged on the professional charges and the search.

Example

A firm acts for a client, Bartok, who is buying a house.

May

1 *The firm pays a mining search fee of £10 + VAT £2. This is not a disbursement for VAT purposes, although the firm will want to show it separately on its bill.*

2 *The firm pays a local land charge search fee of £10 which again is not a disbursement for VAT but will be shown separately on the bill.*

3 *The firm issues a bill. The firm's professional charges are £300 + VAT of £60 but the firm will increase the VAT by £4. The bill will show the two search fees separately from its professional charges.*

Client: Bartok
Matter: Purchase

Date	Details	Business			Client		
		DR	CR	BAL	DR	CR	BAL
May							
1	Mining Search (VAT £2 paid)	10		10DR			
2	Local land charge search (VAT £2 paid)	10		20DR			
30	Profit Costs	300		320DR			
	VAT on £320	64		384DR			

HMRC

Date	**Details**	**Business**		
		DR	**CR**	**BAL**
May				
1	Cash. Bartok. Mining Search	2		
2	Cash. Bartok. Local land search	2		
30	Profit Costs		64	

The Bill will appear as follows

Professional charges	*£300*
Taxable search fees	
Mining Search	*£10*
Local land charge search	*£10*
	£320
VAT @ 20%	*£64*

Where items paid for by solicitors do not fulfil the criteria of disbursements and are included in the supply of legal services, the result is that the client pays VAT on the combined figure. This only has a financial impact on the client if the supplier did not charge VAT. Including the cost in the solicitor's supply of services means that the client pays additional VAT. Of course, if the client is registered for VAT, as the VAT paid is input tax, it will reduce the amount of output tax they pay.

Where the original supplier charged VAT, the solicitor will treat that VAT as input tax. The VAT exclusive amount will be added to the supply and the solicitor will charge output tax. There is no effect on the amount paid by the client. However, where the client is not registered for VAT, they cannot recover the tax paid.

5.3.4 The treatment of disbursements in the firm's accounts

The firm simply passes on the cost to the client. The payment may be for an item which is non-taxable or which includes its own VAT element.

5.3.4.1 Non-taxable disbursements

These are payments for something not subject to VAT, such as exempt supplies and supplies not in the course of business, for example court fees, stamp duty land tax, Land Registry fees, etc.

The firm can pay these out of the client bank account if there is sufficient money in the client bank account. Otherwise, they are paid out of the business bank account.

In neither case does the firm pay VAT to the supplier or charge the client VAT when obtaining reimbursement.

5.3.4.2 Disbursements including a VAT element

These are payments made by the firm to a taxable person in respect of taxable supplies (eg counsel, surveyor, accountant, estate agent, etc). The payment made by the firm will include a VAT element. That VAT element is passed on to the client. The firm does not charge the client any additional VAT.

The difficulty with passing on VAT is that clients who are registered for VAT will want to recover it from HMRC and can do so only if they have a VAT invoice addressed to them. When a firm pays a disbursement that includes VAT on behalf of a client, the supplier may have addressed the invoice to the client or to the firm making the payment.

If the invoice is addressed to the client, it is straightforward. The 'agency' method is used and the VAT inclusive amount is simply passed on to the client.

It is more complicated if the invoice is addressed to the firm. The 'principal' method must be used which requires the solicitor to resupply the service to the client and provide a new VAT invoice.

(1) Agency method

If the invoice is addressed to the client, the supply is treated as made to the client. The firm simply acts as the agent, handing over the money on behalf of the client. If there is sufficient client money standing to the credit of the client, the payment can be made from the client bank account; otherwise, it must be made from the business bank account.

The firm does not separate the supplier's fee and VAT in the firm's accounting records; it simply records the total paid.

The firm must, if asked, send the supplier's tax invoice to the client. If the client is registered for VAT and the supply is in the course or furtherance of a business, the client will use the invoice to recover the input tax.

Example

A firm pays a surveyor's bill on behalf of a client, ABC Co Ltd. The bill is for £1,000 plus £200 VAT. The invoice is addressed to the client and is paid using the agency method.

The firm will simply pay the total sum of £1,200 and not distinguish between the fee and the VAT. Whether the payment is made out of business money or client money, the firm will charge the client £1,200, again without distinguishing between fee and VAT.

Assume that the firm is holding £2,000 on account of costs and is therefore able to make the payment from the client bank account:

Client: ABC Ltd **Matter: Contract Dispute**		**Business account**			**Client account**		
Date	**Details**	**DR**	**CR**	**BAL**	**DR**	**CR**	**BAL**
	Cash. Surveyor				1,200		2,000CR 800CR

Cash account		Business account			Client account		
Date	**Details**	**DR**	**CR**	**BAL**	**DR**	**CR**	**BAL**
	ABC Ltd. Surveyor					1,200	xxx

No entries are made on the firm's HMRC ledger account in relation to the payment.

If the client is registered for VAT, and therefore wants the invoice, the firm must send the client the surveyor's original invoice. The invoice is addressed to the client, and so the client can claim an input.

(2) **Principal method**

If the invoice is addressed to the firm, the supply is treated as made to the firm in the first instance. The firm can claim the supply as an input. The firm, therefore, must use business money to pay the supplier's fees, together with the input tax.

The firm then resupplies the item to the client at the same price.

The firm will charge the client output tax on both the firm's professional charges and the disbursement.

If the client is entitled to a tax invoice, the firm will provide one invoice to cover both the disbursement and the firm's own professional charges.

Example

A firm receives a surveyor's invoice for £200 plus £40 VAT. The firm pays:

	£
Surveyor's fee	*200*
plus input tax	*40*
	240

The fee and the VAT are recorded as separate items on the cash account.

The VAT is recorded on the HMRC account. The tax exclusive amount is recorded on the client ledger account.

When the firm charges the client its professional charges of £400, the bill will include:

	£
Surveyor's fee	*200*
Professional charges	*400*
plus output tax (£40 + £80)	*120*

The surveyor's fee and the VAT are separate items on the bill.

A disbursement paid on the principal method must be paid out of the business bank account, even if there is client money available. This is because the supply is treated as made to the firm and not to the client.

Example

A firm pays a surveyor's bill on behalf of a client, ABC Co Ltd. The bill is for £1,000 plus £200 VAT. The invoice is addressed to the firm and is paid using the principal method.

Assume that the firm is holding £2,000 on account of costs.

The firm will have to pay the disbursement from the business bank account even though client money is held for the client. The entries will be as follows.

Client: ABC Ltd **Matter: Contract Dispute**		**Business account**			**Client account**		
Date	**Details**	**DR**	**CR**	**BAL**	**DR**	**CR**	**BAL**
							2,000CR
	Cash. Surveyor (VAT £200 paid)	1,000		1,000DR			

HMRC account

Date	**Details**	**DR**	**CR**	**BAL**
	Cash. Surveyor	200		XXX

Cash account		**Business account**			**Client account**		
Date	**Details**	**DR**	**CR**	**BAL**	**DR**	**CR**	**BAL**
	ABC Ltd. Surveyor VAT		1,000 200	XXX XXX			XXX

When the firm charges the client for the work done, the VAT on the profit costs is increased by the VAT on the disbursement. Assume the firm charges profit costs of £600.

Client: ABC Ltd Matter: Contract Dispute		Business account			Client account		
Date	**Details**	**DR**	**CR**	**BAL**	**DR**	**CR**	**BAL**
							2,000CR
	Cash. Surveyor (VAT £200 paid)	1,000		1,000DR			
	Profit costs	600		1,600DR			
	VAT (£200+£120)	320		1,920DR			

HMRC account

Date	Details	DR	CR	BAL
	Cash. Surveyor	200		xxx
	Client		320	xxx

Profit costs

Date	Details	DR	CR	BAL
	Client		600	xxx

CHECKLIST ON PRINCIPAL METHOD

(1) Identify that the disbursement is to be treated on the principal basis – if the invoice is addressed to the firm, it will be treated on the principal basis.

(2) CR the disbursement and the VAT on it to cash account business section – it is common, but not essential, to show the two elements separately.

(3) DR VAT to HMRC ledger.

DR VAT exclusive amount to client ledger account business section.

Make a memorandum note in the 'Details' column of the client ledger of the amount of VAT which must be added to the VAT charged to the client when an invoice is issued.

(4) When a bill is issued, add the VAT on the principal method disbursement to the VAT on the professional charges and make the normal entries for delivery of a bill.

DR client ledger account business section, with VAT and costs as two separate amounts.

CR the profit costs account with costs.

CR HMRC account with total VAT charged.

5.3.4.3 Counsel's fees – concessionary treatment

Normally, counsel's fee notes are addressed to the firm and therefore would have to be treated on the principal basis. However, a concessionary treatment for counsel's fees was agreed between HMRC, The Law Society and the Bar when VAT was first introduced, and was published in the *Law Society Gazette*, 4 April 1973. The concession is not set out in any HMRC manual or VAT notice.

The firm is allowed to alter the fee note so that it is addressed to the client. It is then treated on the agency basis. The firm must give the fee note to the client so that the client can reclaim the input tax. The firm should keep a photocopy of the amended receipted fee note in case the fee note needs to be dealt with in an assessment of costs.

On 31 August 2021 the Law Society confirmed that the concession still stands, but that it is undertaking a review to consider whether it should be withdrawn.

Summary

- Persons registered for VAT must charge customers/clients VAT at zero, standard or reduced rate on all taxable supplies of goods and services made in the course or furtherance of the business and can recover any VAT charged to the business.
- Firms must charge VAT on their supply of legal services but do not charge VAT on disbursements paid on behalf of their clients as these are not part of the supply of legal services. However, to qualify as a disbursement, the supply must be for the client's use and not for the solicitor. If the payment is for an item required by the solicitor to provide legal services, the item is not a disbursement. It is part of the solicitor's fee for providing the service. The solicitor must charge VAT on the item.
- The cost of a disbursement is simply passed on to the client.
- if the disbursement incudes an element of VAT charged by the original supplier, the firm will treat the disbursement either on the agency basis or on the principal basis. The choice of basis is governed by to whom the invoice is addressed.
- If an invoice is addressed to the client, the firm treats the disbursement on the agency basis:
    - the whole payment is recorded on the cash account and client ledger account without distinguishing the VAT
    - the firm can use client money to make the payment if there is sufficient available; if not, the firm uses its own money
    - the firm must give the client the original supplier's invoice if the client is registered for VAT.
- If an invoice is addressed to the firm, the firm treats the disbursement on the principal basis:
    - the whole payment is recorded on the cash account, the VAT is recorded on the HMRC account and the VAT exclusive amount is recorded on the client ledger account;
    - the VAT will be charged to the client when the firm bills the client;
    - the firm uses its own money to make the payment even if client money is available;
    - the firm must give the client a VAT invoice covering both the professional charges of the firm and the VAT on the disbursement; and
    - in the case of counsel's fee note the firm is allowed to cross out the firm's name and add the client's; the invoice can then be dealt with on the agency basis.

Sample questions

Question 1

During an accounting period, a firm of solicitors bills its clients for total professional charges of £400,000 plus VAT of £80,000. In the same accounting period, the firm buys a computer for £10,000 plus VAT of £2,000. The firm is registered for VAT purposes.

How much is the firm required to pay to HMRC in respect of VAT at the end of the accounting period?

A £80,000.

B £2,000.

C £82,000.

D £78,000.

E Nothing.

Answer

Option D is correct. The firm has been charged £2,000 input tax on the supply of goods for the purposes of its business. The firm can therefore deduct the £2,000 from the £80,000 output tax which it accounts for to HMRC.

Question 2

A firm of solicitors is registered for VAT purposes. The firm is refurbishing its offices. As part of that process the firm sells some items of redundant office furniture. The buyer is not registered for VAT purposes.

Must the firm charge VAT on the sale price?

A Yes, because the sale is made for a cash consideration.

B Yes, because the sale is made in the course of the firm's business.

C No, because this is an exempt supply.

D No, because this is not a supply of legal services.

E No, because the buyer is not a taxable person.

Answer

Option B is correct. The firm must charge VAT on any supply made in the course of its business, not just on its supply of legal services; option D therefore is wrong. The sale of furniture does not fall within the category of exempt supplies (with the result that option C is wrong). Option A is wrong; the charging of VAT on the supply of goods is not dependent on the payment of cash consideration. The taxable status of the buyer is only relevant on the question of reclaiming input tax; option E is therefore wrong.

Question 3

A firm of solicitors is acting for a client in a litigation matter. The firm is currently holding £600 in its client bank account for the client generally on account of costs. The firm receives an invoice from an enquiry agent for charges of £400 plus VAT in connection with the client's matter. The enquiry agent's invoice is addressed to the firm.

Which of the following best explains which bank account the firm should use to pay the invoice?

A Client, because the firm is holding sufficient funds on the client's behalf.

B Client, because the invoice relates to the client's matter.

C Business, because the firm has not yet delivered its bill.

D Business, because the invoice is addressed to the firm.

E Business, because the client has not given instructions for the payment to be made from the client bank account.

Answer

Option D is correct. As the enquiry agent's invoice is addressed to the firm, the principal method must be used. The firm's own money must therefore be used to pay the invoice even if there is money available in the client bank account.

6 Special Accounting Entries

SQE1 syllabus

This chapter will help you to achieve the SQE1 Assessment Specification in relation to Functioning Legal Knowledge concerned with the core principles of double entry bookkeeping and the SRA Accounts Rules on:

- requirement to pay promptly money into a client account;
- circumstances in which client money may be withheld from a client account;
- withdrawals from client account;
- duty to correct breaches of the Rules promptly on discovery;
- requirement to keep accurate records to include reduction of bills;
- accounting entries required.

Note that for SQE1, candidates are not usually required to recall specific case names or cite statutory or regulatory authorities.

Learning outcomes

By the end of this chapter you will be able to apply relevant core principles of double entry bookkeeping and the SRA Accounts Rules appropriately and effectively, at the level of a competent newly qualified solicitor in practice, to realistic client-based ethical problems and situations in the following areas:

- Cheques made out to third parties;
- Dishonoured cheques;
- Abatements;
- Bad debts;
- Petty cash;
- Insurance commission.

6.1 Introduction

All firms providing legal services will carry out a range of common transactions every day and record them appropriately in their accounting records. These common accounting entries were dealt with in Chapter 3. However, more transactions may occur from time to time.

This chapter looks at:

- cheques made out to the client or to third parties;
- dishonoured cheques;
- abatements;
- bad debts;
- petty cash;
- insurance commission.

6.2 Receipt of a cheque made out to the client or a third party

If a firm receives a cheque made out, not to the firm, but to the client (or a third party), the cheque cannot be paid into a firm's bank account. The firm is not the payee.

The firm's only obligation is to forward the cheque to the payee without delay. The firm has not received client money because the cheque is not 'money' as far as the firm is concerned; it is a piece of paper which the firm cannot turn into cash. As the firm has not received client money, there is no obligation under Rule 8.1(a) to record the event on the client ledger account and cash account. However, the firm will want to keep a written record on the correspondence file.

As a precaution, many firms will have a special control account where all cheques received by the firm will be recorded irrespective of the payee. This is not required by the Rules but it helps to prevent cheques being overlooked.

6.3 Dishonoured cheques

There is nothing in the Rules to prevent a firm drawing against a cheque which has been paid into the client bank account but which has not yet been cleared. However, if that cheque is then dishonoured, there will be a breach of Rule 5.3. More money has been taken from the client bank account than is held for the particular client. Money belonging to other clients will, therefore, have been used to make the payment. Under Rule 6.1 any breaches of the Rules must be corrected promptly upon discovery, and any money improperly withdrawn from a client account must be immediately replaced. Here, the firm will have to make good the shortfall by transferring its own money to the client bank account.

Example

On 1 March, a solicitor receives a cheque for £500 on account of costs from a client, Visinoni.

On 2 March, the solicitor pays a court fee of £100 out of the client bank account on behalf of Visinoni.

On 4 March, the bank informs the solicitor that Visinoni's cheque for £500 has been dishonoured.

First the solicitor must make entries to reverse the apparent receipt on 1 March. Then the solicitor must deal with the consequences of the payment from the client bank account.

Because the firm had no money for Visinoni, when the solicitor made the £100 payment, the solicitor must have used £100 belonging to another client for the benefit of Visinoni. This is in breach of Rule 5.3. In compliance with Rule 6.1 the solicitor must, therefore, transfer £100 from the business bank account to the client bank account to remedy the breach of the rules.

On 7 March, Visinoni tells the solicitor that there are now sufficient funds to meet the cheque. He asks the solicitor to re-present the cheque. The solicitor does so on 7 March and it is met.

When the solicitor re-presents the cheque, the client now owes the firm £100. So, the receipt is a mixture of business and client money. This means that the solicitor can either split the cheque, or pay the whole amount into one account and transfer funds to the other account promptly (Rule 4.2). If the solicitor pays the whole £500 into the client bank account, the £100 must be transferred to the business bank account promptly.

March

1 *The money is client money (Rule 2.1) and is paid into the client bank account (Rule 2.3):*

CR Visinoni ledger account
DR Cash account } *Client section*

2 *The solicitor makes the payment from the client bank account even though the cheque from Visinoni has not yet been cleared:*

DR Visinoni ledger account
CR Cash account } *Client section*

4 *To record the dishonouring, the solicitor must make entries reversing those made when the cheque was received:*

DR Visinoni ledger account
CR Cash account } *Client section*

This results in a DR balance of £100 on Visinoni's ledger account and this is a breach of Rule 5.3. Effectively, the firm has used client money on behalf of a client for whom the firm was not holding any.

4 *The solicitor must make an immediate transfer of £100 from the business bank account to the client bank account to rectify the breach.*

Withdrawal from business account:

DR Visinoni ledger account
CR Cash account } *Business section*

Receipt into client account:

CR Visinoni ledger account
DR Cash account } *Client section*

7 *When the cheque is re-presented the solicitor can, under Rule 4.2, either pay the whole amount into one bank account, or, as in this example, split it so that £100 goes into the business bank account and £400 into the client bank account.*

If the cheque is split:

£100 business money

CR Visinoni ledger account
DR Cash account } *Business section*

£400 Client money:

CR Visinoni ledger account } *Client section*
DR Cash account

Client: Visinoni **Matter: Miscellaneous**		**Business account**			**Client account**		
Date	**Details**	**DR**	**CR**	**BAL**	**DR**	**CR**	**BAL**
March							
1	Cash. From Visinoni. On account					500	500CR
2	Cash. Court fee				100		400CR
4	Cash. Visinoni's cheque returned				500		100DR
7	Cash. Transfer from business account to rectify breach	100		100DR		100	—
	Cash. Visinoni's cheque re-presented		100	—		400	400CR

Cash account		**Business account**			**Client account**		
Date	**Details**	**DR**	**CR**	**BAL**	**DR**	**CR**	**BAL**
March							
1	Visinoni				500		xxx
2	Visinoni					100	
4	Visinoni					500	
	Visinoni		100		100		
7	Visinoni	100			400		

A well-run firm will operate a system which makes it impossible to draw against a client's cheque before it has cleared.

6.4 Abatement

Clients may complain that the amount of their bill is too high. Sometimes, the firm may decide to reduce, or abate, the costs. HMRC allows the output tax charged on the bill to be reduced proportionately.

In order to record the abatement, the entries made on the profit costs and HMRC account when the bill was sent are reversed to the extent of the abatement. The firm must also send the client a VAT credit note.

DR Profit costs account } with the reduction
DR HMRC account

CR Client ledger account (business section) with the reduction in professional charges and VAT.

Example

A firm sends a bill for £600 plus VAT to a client, Rana, on 4 May. Rana queries the bill. On 6 May the firm agrees to reduce the bill by £100 plus VAT.

Client: Rana **Matter: Miscellaneous**		**Business account**			**Client account**		
Date	**Details**	**DR**	**CR**	**BAL**	**DR**	**CR**	**BAL**
May							
4	Profit costs	600		600DR			
	VAT	120		720DR			
6	Profit costs - abatement		100	620DR			
	VAT - abatement		20	600DR			

Profit costs account

Date	Details	DR	CR	BAL
May				
4	Rana		600	600CR
6	Rana - abatement	100		500CR

HMRC account

Date	Details	DR	CR	BAL
May				
4	Rana		120	120CR
6	Rana	20		100CR

As an alternative, the firm may debit abatements to a separate abatements account. At the end of the accounting period, the debit balance on the abatements account is transferred to the debit side of the profit costs account.

6.5 Bad debts

From time to time, a firm will realise that a client is not going to pay the amount owing to the firm. The firm will have to write off the amount owing for its professional charges and VAT and for any disbursements paid from the business bank account.

CR Client's ledger account, business section } with the whole amount
DR Bad debts account

VAT relief is available once the debt has been outstanding for at least six months since the date payment was due. In this case, the firm will be entitled to a refund from HMRC.

CR Bad debts account with amount of VAT

DR HMRC with amount of VAT

Example

A firm sends a bill for professional charges of £400 plus VAT to a client, Clark, on 9 April. On 6 June, the firm writes off Clark's debt.

Six months after the due date of payment of Clark's bill (31 October), the firm becomes entitled to VAT bad debt relief.

Client: Clark **Matter: Miscellaneous**		**Business account**			**Client account**		
Date	**Details**	**DR**	**CR**	**BAL**	**DR**	**CR**	**BAL**
April							
9	Profit costs	400		400DR			
	VAT	80		480DR			
June							
6	Bad debts		480	—			

Profit costs account

Date	**Details**	**DR**	**CR**	**BAL**
April				
9	Clark		400	400CR

HMRC account

Date	**Details**	**DR**	**CR**	**BAL**
April				
9	Clark		80	80CR
Oct				
31	Bad debts. VAT Relief	80		—

Bad debts account

Date	Details	DR	CR	BAL
June 6	Clark	480		480DR
Oct 31	HMRC. VAT Relief		80	400DR

6.6 Petty cash

Any firm will need some petty cash on the premises to meet small cash payments. When cash is withdrawn from the bank for petty cash:

CR Cash – business section

DR Petty cash account

When a payment is made, for example a roll of sticky tape is bought:

CR Petty cash account

DR appropriate ledger account, for example Sundries

A firm will sometimes make a payment from petty cash on behalf of a client. The CR entry will be made on the petty cash account, not on the main cash account. The firm will want to DR the client ledger account to show that the client now owes the firm for the expense incurred. The DR entry must be made on the business section of the client ledger account even if client money is held for the client. This is because petty cash is business money. Therefore, by deciding to use petty cash, the firm has elected to use business money on behalf of the client.

Example

A firm holds £200 in the client bank account for Assi. The firm pays £20 expenses to an expert witness from petty cash.

Client: Assi **Matter: Miscellaneous**		**Business account**			**Client account**		
Date	**Details**	**DR**	**CR**	**BAL**	**DR**	**CR**	**BAL**
	Cash. Received on account					200	200CR
	Petty cash. Expert witness	20		20DR			

The corresponding credit entry will be on the petty cash account, not on the cash account.

6.7 Insurance commission

Firms providing legal services may be offered commission from insurance companies or sellers of financial products. Where the firm is entitled to retain the commission, it represents an additional source of income; the firm will have a commission received account to which receipts are credited and a ledger account in the name of each company paying commission.

However, it will be relatively rare for the firm to be entitled to retain commission. Paragraph 5.1 of the SRA Code of Conduct for Firms requires those regulated by the SRA to 'properly account' to clients for any financial benefit received as a result of client instructions (see **Ethics and Professional Conduct**).

Where a financial benefit has been received as a result of acting for a client, 'properly accounting' is likely to be:

- paying it to the client;
- offsetting it against fees; or
- keeping it only where the firm can justify keeping it, has told the client the amount of the benefit (or an approximation if the exact amount is not known) and the client has agreed to the firm keeping it.

Most firms would not wish to retain commission in any event. Retaining commission would take the firm outside the exemption allowing professional firms to avoid regulation by the Financial Reporting Council in relation to investment business (see **Legal Services**).

Summary

- Cheques which are not made out to the firm cannot be paid into the firm's bank account. The cheque does not represent money in the firm's hands. The firm must forward the cheque to the payee and does not need to record the receipt and payment in the accounts as there is no dealing with client money.
- A firm can draw against a client's cheque before it has cleared. However, this is not advisable. If the client cheque is dishonoured, the firm will have breached the Rules and will have to remedy the breach by transferring sufficient cash from the business to the client bank account to cover the payment.
- If a firm reduces the amount charged for profit costs, the VAT is also reduced.
- If a client's debt is written off, the firm will lose the amount charged for profit costs plus any disbursements paid from the business bank account. VAT bad debts relief is available once the debt has been outstanding for six months.
- Petty cash is business money. Any payment made for a client using petty cash is a payment of business money.
- A firm will usually account to a client for commission received as a result of acting for a client.

Sample questions

Question 1

A solicitor delivers a bill to a client for professional charges of £1,000 plus VAT. The client complains that the bill is too high. The solicitor agrees to reduce the bill by 10%.

Which of the following best describes how the reduction should be recorded on the client ledger account?

A CR (Business section) Profit costs - abatement £100.
CR (Business section) VAT - abatement £20.

B CR (Business section) Profit costs - abatement £120.

C CR (Business section) Profit costs - abatement £100.
DR (Business section) VAT - abatement £20.

D CR (Client section) Profit costs - abatement £100.
CR (Client section) VAT - abatement £20.

E DR (Business section) Profit costs - abatement £100.
DR (Business section) VAT - abatement £20.

Answer

Option A is correct. In order to record the abatement, the entries made on the business section of the client ledger account at the time that the bill was issued are reversed to the extent of the abatement. Two CR entries are needed to show the reductions on profit costs and VAT. The corresponding DR entries are on the profit costs and HMRC accounts respectively.

Question 2

A solicitor is instructed by a new client in a litigation matter. At the initial interview the solicitor asks the client to pay £500 generally on account of costs and disbursements. The client says that they will let the solicitor have a cheque for that sum within the next week. It is now five days after the initial interview and the client has not yet made any payment to the solicitor. The solicitor needs to pay a court fee of £100 on the client's behalf.

Which of the following best explains which bank account the solicitor should use to pay the £100?

A Client, because disbursements must always be paid from the client bank account.

B Client, because the client's cheque for £500 will arrive within the next two days.

C Business, because the firm is holding insufficient funds on this client's behalf.

D Business, because this is a payment of petty cash.

E Business, because disbursements must always be paid from the business bank account.

Answer

Option C is correct. Generally, disbursements can be paid from either the business bank account or the client bank account, as appropriate; options A and E are accordingly wrong. Option B is wrong; here the payment cannot be made from the client bank account because the firm is not holding any money for this client (Rule 5.3). It is not a payment from petty cash and option D therefore is wrong.

Question 3

A solicitor delivers a bill to a client for professional charges of £1,000 and VAT of £200. The client sends the solicitor a cheque, made payable to the firm, for £1,200 in payment of the bill, but the accompanying letter instructs the solicitor not to pay in the cheque until the client confirms that there are sufficient funds in their bank account for the cheque to clear.

Should the solicitor pay the cheque into the firm's client bank account?

A Yes, because client money cannot be withheld from the client bank account.

B Yes, because the firm is entitled to be paid for the work it has done.

C No, because the cheque may be dishonoured.

D No, because this is not a receipt of client money.

E No, because the client's instructions have been given in writing.

Answer

Option D is correct. Money received in payment of a bill is not client money and so cannot be paid into the client bank account.

7 Interest

SQE1 syllabus

This chapter will enable you to achieve the SQE1 Assessment Specification in relation to Functioning Legal Knowledge concerned with the core principles of double entry bookkeeping and the SRA Accounts Rules on:

- requirement to pay interest on client money;
- accounting entries required.

Note that for SQE1, candidates are not usually required to recall specific case names or cite statutory or regulatory authorities.

Learning outcomes

By the end of this chapter you will be able to apply relevant core principles of double entry bookkeeping and the SRA Accounts Rules appropriately and effectively, at the level of a competent newly qualified solicitor in practice, to realistic client-based ethical problems and situations in the following areas:

- The circumstances in which a client is entitled to interest on client money;
- The two methods of accounting for interest;
- The advantages and disadvantages of each method of accounting for interest;
- How interest is calculated;
- The accounting entries required to record the payment of interest.

7.1 Introduction

Solicitors may hold money belonging to other people for long periods of time. Inevitably the question will arise as to whether those people are entitled to be paid a sum in lieu of the interest they might otherwise be earning on that money. SRA Principles 5 and 7 require those providing regulated services to act with integrity and in the best interests of the client. In order to comply with those obligations, it will frequently be appropriate for firms to account to clients for interest on client money held.

This chapter looks at:

- the obligation to account;
- the use of a separate designated deposit client account;
- the use of a general client bank account.

7.2 The obligation to account

7.2.1 The obligation

Paragraph 1.2 of the SRA Code of Conduct for Solicitors, RELs and RFLs requires: 'You do not abuse your position by taking unfair advantage of clients or others.' Paragraph 4.1 of the Code requires: 'You properly account to clients for any financial benefit you receive as a result of their instructions, except where they have agreed otherwise.' Based on these general principles, it would clearly be wrong for firms to earn interest on money held in the client bank account without accounting for the benefit to clients.

The Rules go beyond general principles and impose a specific requirement as to interest. Rule 7.1 of the Rules states that you must 'account to clients or third parties for a fair sum of interest on any client money held by you on their behalf, unless you have reached a separate agreement with your client'. Rule 7.2 states that you 'may by a written agreement come to a different arrangement with the client or the third party for whom the money is held as to the payment of interest', but you must provide the client or third party with 'sufficient information to enable them to give informed consent'.

The Rules do not stipulate when interest is to be paid nor how it is to be calculated. Instead the onus is on individual firms to set their own policy on the circumstances in which it is fair to account to clients for interest and how such interest is to be calculated.

A policy is likely to provide that interest will be accounted for unless it is less than a stated figure, say, £20. The figure will need to be set at a reasonable level. What is reasonable will depend on a number of factors, including the nature of the firm's practice. A figure of £20 might be appropriate for a firm acting primarily for private individuals. However, a higher figure is likely to be more appropriate for a corporate client base. Corporate clients are more likely to be willing to waive very small interest payments if for no other reason than they will incur administrative costs in processing them. Although a firm should have a general policy on interest in place, it is permissible to agree a different arrangement with an individual client.

The terms of the policy should be drawn to the client's attention at the start of the retainer unless it is inappropriate to do so, for example where the client has a continuing relationship with the firm.

As part of its consultation on client money in legal services, the SRA is considering changing the Rules on interest. Proposals under discussion include preventing firms retaining interest on money held for clients.

7.2.2 Methods of dealing with interest

There are two possible ways of dealing with interest. Firms can choose to pay client money either (1) into a general client bank account or (2) into a separate deposit bank account designated for money of that particular client (a 'separate designated deposit bank account').

Whichever method is chosen, the requirement under the Rules is the same: the interest allowed must be a 'fair sum'.

Firms will usually open a separate designated deposit bank account for a particular client's money when they recognise that they will be holding a substantial amount for a significant time and simply want to pass on to the client all the interest allowed by the bank. In the past, the income tax rules applying to bank interest made it impracticable for firms to retain any part of the interest earned. Although a simpler tax regime is now in place whereby banks and building societies pay all interest gross, it is likely that firms will continue to account to clients for all interest earned on money in specially designated accounts given the obligation to act in the client's best interests.

Where a client's money is left in the general client bank account, the firm has to decide by reference to its policy whether to allow interest and how to calculate it. The sum decided upon will be allowed from the business bank account and is, in effect, an expense of the business – a well-run firm will cover the expense by earning interest on client money and having that interest paid into its business bank account (see **7.2.3**).

7.2.3 Factors affecting the choice of method

When the firm opens a separate designated deposit bank account, the bank calculates the amount and pays the amount of interest earned. If such an account is not opened, the firm has to pay an appropriate amount in lieu of interest from the business bank account. It might seem, therefore, that it is always preferable to open a separate designated deposit bank account. However, this is not so.

A firm which opened a separate designated deposit bank account for every client for whom money was held would have an enormous number of different client bank accounts, and this would be administratively inconvenient.

Moreover, solicitors are allowed under the Solicitors Act 1974 to put client money held in a general client bank account on deposit and keep any interest earned over and above what is required to be paid under the Rules. In general, the more money placed on deposit, the higher the rate of interest earned. The firm only has to pay the client the rate that is fair in relation to the amount held *for that client*. The result is that the firm may earn more interest on client money than is paid out to clients. This is likely to encourage the firm to use the second method.

7.3 Use of a separate designated deposit bank account

7.3.1 The nature of the account

The firm simply opens a deposit account at the bank designated with the name of the client or third party and pays the client money into it. Unlike the general client bank account, this account will be reserved for money of the particular client or third party. The firm will account to the client for the interest allowed by the bank.

Where a firm opens separate designated deposit bank accounts, it will need to ensure that the recording requirements of Rule 8.1 are complied with:

(a) The client's ledger account must show receipts and payments of client money dealt with through the separate designated deposit bank account. This will require either a separate ledger account for designated deposit bank account transactions or separate columns on the ordinary client ledger account.

(b) The firm's cash account must include details of receipts and payments of client money dealt with through the separate designated deposit bank account. This could be a separate cash account for each designated deposit bank account or, more likely, a combined cash account showing transactions on all the designated deposit bank accounts.

The disadvantage of this method is that the firm loses the opportunity to benefit from interest earned by client money.

7.3.2 Accounting entries

The firm will instruct the bank to open a deposit bank account – the separate designated deposit bank account. The client money will either be paid directly into the separate designated deposit bank account, or, if it is currently held in the general client bank account, the firm will instruct the bank to transfer the appropriate amount from the (current) client bank account. The firm will record the receipt into the separate designated deposit bank account by making a DR entry on the deposit cash account. Entries are also needed on the client ledger accounts to show what has happened to the money.

The firm may choose to have additional columns on the client ledger to record receipts and payments through the separate designated deposit bank account. The client ledger would then look like this:

Client
Matter:

Date	Details	Busines			Client			Client-deposit		
		DR	CR	BAL	DR	CR	BAL	DR	CR	BAL

When a separate ledger account is used, the business columns are normally redundant as there is already a client ledger account showing dealings with business money. In the following examples the business columns on separate ledger accounts are shaded to indicate that they will not be used.

When transferring money from the general client bank account to a separate designated deposit bank account, there are two stages:

(1) To record a payment out of the general client bank account:

CR Cash } Client section
DR Client ledger account (1)

(2) To record a receipt into the separate designated deposit bank account:

CR Client ledger account (2) (or additional deposit column on Client ledger account (1))

DR Deposit cash account

If money is received and paid straight into a separate designated deposit bank account, step 1 is not required.

The bank will pay interest earned into the separate designated deposit bank account. The interest is recorded as a CR on the client's new ledger account and as a DR on the deposit cash account.

Banks often do not allow payments directly from deposit accounts. Where this is the case, the total sum including interest must be transferred from the separate designated deposit bank account to the general client bank account. However, it is not necessary to wait for the funds to actually be received into the general client bank account before making the payment.

Example

A solicitor acts for a client, Dash Ltd, which is owed £2,200 by Bingley. The solicitor writes to Bingley and receives a cheque from him for the money owed on 3 April. On 4 April, Dash Ltd tells the solicitor to hold the money for five weeks until 9 May. The solicitor puts the money on deposit in a separate designated deposit bank account. On 9 May, the solicitor tells the bank to close the account. The bank has allowed £18 interest. The £2,218 is transferred to the general client bank account. The solicitor sends Dash Ltd the £2,218.

April

3 *The money is received as client money and paid into the general client bank account.*

CR Dash Ltd (debt collection) ledger account } *Client section*
DR Cash account

4 *The bank will transfer the cash from the firm's general client bank account to the separate designated deposit bank account. An entry must be made on the deposit cash account (DCA) to record the additional funds held in the separate designated deposit bank account, and a new client ledger account (or additional deposit section on the old client ledger) to show that funds are held for Dash in a separate designated deposit bank account.*

CR Cash account } *Client section*
DR Dash Ltd (debt collection) ledger account

DR Deposit cash account

CR Dash Ltd (money held on deposit) ledger account

May

9 *The interest must be dealt with first. The interest has been earned on behalf of Dash Ltd and belongs to Dash Ltd. It is client money and the bank will pay it into the separate designated deposit bank account.*

DR DCA with interest

CR Dash Ltd (money held on deposit) ledger account with interest

The total must be paid out from the separate designated deposit bank account.

CR DCA

DR Dash Ltd (money held on deposit) ledger account

The total is received into the general client bank account.

DR Cash account } *Client section*
CR Dash Ltd (debt collection) ledger account

The solicitor will now pay Dash Ltd the total sum the firm is holding on its behalf.

CR Cash account

DR Dash Ltd (debt collection) ledger account

Client: Dash Ltd (1) **Matter: Debt collection**		**Business account**			**Client account**		
Date	**Details**	**DR**	**CR**	**BAL**	**DR**	**CR**	**BAL**
April							
3	Cash. Bingley					2,200	2,200CR
4	Cash. On deposit				2,200		—
May							
9	Cash. Off deposit					2,218	2,218CR
	Cash. Returned				2,218		—

Client: Dash Ltd (2) **Matter: Money held on deposit**		**Business account**			**Client account**		
Date	**Details**	**DR**	**CR**	**BAL**	**DR**	**CR**	**BAL**
April							
4	Deposit cash. A/c opened					2,200	2,200CR
May							
9	Deposit cash interest					18	2,218CR
	Deposit cash. A/c closed				2,218		—

Client: Cash account		**Business account**			**Client account**		
Date	**Details**	**DR**	**CR**	**BAL**	**DR**	**CR**	**BAL**
April				XXX			XXX
3	Dash Ltd (1). Bingley				2,200		
4	Dash Ltd (1). On deposit					2,200	
May							
9	Dash Ltd (1). Off deposit				2,218		
	Dash Ltd. Returned					2,218	

Deposit cash account (DCA)		**Business account**			**Client account**		
Date	**Details**	**DR**	**CR**	**BAL**	**DR**	**CR**	**BAL**
April							
4	Dash Ltd (2). A/c opened				2,200		XXX
May							
9	Dash Ltd (2). Interest				18		
	Dash Ltd. A/c closed					2,218	

As an alternative to having a separate client ledger account, the entries can be shown on a deposit section on the existing client ledger account:

Client: Dash Ltd Matter: Debt collection		Business	Client			Client – deposit		
Date	Details		DR	CR	BAL	DR	CR	BAL
April								
3	Cash. Bingley			2,200	2,200CR			
4	Cash. On deposit		2,200		—			
4	Deposit cash. A/c opened						2,200	2,200CR
May								
9	Deposit cash. Interest						18	2,218CR —
	Deposit cash. A/c closed					2,218		
	Cash. Off deposit			2,218	2,218CR			
	Cash. Returned		2,218		—			

Client: Cash account		Business account			Client account		
Date	Details	DR	CR	BAL	DR	CR	BAL
April				xxx			xxx
3	Dash Ltd. Bingley				2,200		
4	Dash Ltd. On deposit					2,200	
May							
9	Dash Ltd. Off deposit				2,218		
	Dash Ltd. Returned					2,218	

Deposit cash account (DCA)		Business account			Client account		
Date	Details	DR	CR	BAL	DR	CR	BAL
April							
4	Dash Ltd. A/c opened				2,200		xxx
May							
9	Dash Ltd. Interest				18		
	Dash Ltd. A/c closed					2,218	

7.4 Use of the general client bank account

7.4.1 The general client bank account

A firm may decide to hold client money in its general client bank account rather than in a separate designated deposit bank account. If that is the case then under Rule 7.1, based on its policy, the firm must calculate a fair sum and allow it to the client.

The disadvantage of this method is that the firm has to calculate how much would have been earned in respect of each individual client to whom the rules apply. Also, at first sight, it appears that the firm will be out of pocket. However, as explained at **7.2.3**, this is not necessarily the case.

A well-organised firm will always put a proportion of its client money on deposit in a general deposit bank account. It will then be entitled to keep the interest earned on that general deposit bank account. Provided the firm organises its bank accounts sensibly, it should earn more interest on its general deposit bank account than it has to pay to individual clients. A firm can never put all of its client money on deposit since it must ensure that it has sufficient client money readily available to meet all day-to-day payments for clients.

Often, the amount allowed in interest will simply reduce the amount that the client has to pay the firm for the services provided. However, if the client has already paid, the firm may actually send a cheque.

7.4.2 Accounting entries

Using this method, the interest payment is an expense of the business and will be recorded on an interest payable ledger account. It is equivalent to the firm paying any other business expense, such as electricity or wages.

The business money dealing will be recorded in a business cash account and on the business section of the client ledger account. If the money is transferred from the business bank account to the client bank account and held for the client, entries must be made on the client ledger account and cash account to record the cash transfer from the business to client bank account.

Example

A solicitor acts for a client, Dash Ltd, which is owed £2,200 by Bingley. The solicitor writes to Bingley and receives a cheque from him for the money owed on 3 April. On 4 April, Dash Ltd tells the solicitor to hold the money for five weeks until 9 May. On 9 May, the firm decides to allow £18 interest. The solicitor sends Dash Ltd the £2,218.

April

3 The money is received as client money and paid into the general client bank account.

Entries:

CR Dash Ltd (debt collection) ledger accounts } *Client section*
DR Cash account }

May

9 The firm allows Dash Ltd £18 interest, and therefore must account to Dash Ltd for £2,218. This can be achieved in one of two ways.

Method 1

Send two cheques: one drawn on the business bank account for the £18 interest, and the other drawn on the client bank account for the £2,200.

Entries must be made on the client ledger business section to record the dealing with business money.

To record £18 owed to the client in interest:

DR interest payable ledger account } *Business section*

CR Dash Ltd ledger account

To record £18 business cash sent to client:

DR Dash Ltd ledger account } *Business section*

CR Cash account

To record £2,200 client cash sent to client:

DR Dash Ltd ledger account } *Client section*

CR Cash account

Client: Dash Ltd
Matter: Debt collection

Date	**Details**	**Business account**			**Client account**		
		DR	**CR**	**BAL**	**DR**	**CR**	**BAL**
April							
3	Cash. Bingley					2,200	2,200CR
May							
9	Interest payable		18	18CR			
9	Cash. Interest	18		—			
9	Cash. Returned				2,200		—

Cash account

Date	**Details**	**Business account**			**Client account**		
			CR	**BAL**	**DR**	**CR**	**BAL**
April							
3	Dash Ltd. Bingley				2,200		
May							
9	Dash Ltd. Interest		18				
9	Dash Ltd. Returned					2,200	

Interest payable account

Date	**Details**	**Business account**		
		DR	**CR**	**BAL**
May				
9	Dash Ltd.	18		18DR

Method 2

Transfer the £18 from the business bank account to the client bank account, and then send Dash Ltd one cheque drawn on the client bank account for £2,218. In this case, additional entries must be made on the client section of the client ledger and on the client section of the cash account to show that money has been held for the client in the client bank account.

To record £18 owed to client in interest:

DR Interest payable ledger account *CR Dash Ltd ledger account*	} *Business section*

To record £18 business cash paid out of the business bank account:

DR Dash Ltd ledger account *CR Cash*	} *Business section*

To record £18 received into client bank account:

CR Dash Ltd ledger account *DR Cash account*	} *Client section*

To record payment to Dash Ltd of £2,218 from client bank account:

DR Dash Ltd ledger account *CR Cash account*	} *Client section*

Client: Dash Ltd
Matter: Debt collection

Date	**Details**	**Business account**			**Client account**		
		DR	**CR**	**BAL**	**DR**	**CR**	**BAL**
April							
3	Cash					2,200	2,200CR
May							
9	Interest payable		18	18CR			
9	Cash. Interest	18		—		18	2,218CR
9	Cash. Returned				2,218		—

Cash account

Date	**Details**	**Business account**			**Client account**		
		DR	**CR**	**BAL**	**DR**	**CR**	**BAL**
April							XXX
3	Dash Ltd. Bingley				2,200		
May							
9	Dash Ltd. Interest		18	XXX			
9	Dash Ltd. Interest				18		XXX
9	Dash Ltd. Returned					2,218	XXX

Interest payable account

Date	Details	Business account		
		DR	CR	BAL
May 9	Dash Ltd. Bingley	18		18DR

Summary

- Rule 7.1 creates the obligation to account to clients and third parties for a fair sum of interest on client money held on their behalf by firms providing legal services. This is subject to the proviso that the firm may agree a different arrangement in writing with the client/third party as to the payment of interest.
- It is for each firm to adopt its own policy for determining what constitutes a fair sum of interest.
- A firm can use one of two methods to meet the obligation to account for interest:
  - open a separate deposit account designated with the name of the client and account to the client for all the interest earned on the account; or
  - pay the client interest from the business bank account. The amount due is calculated by reference to the firm's policy and must be a fair sum.
- The Solicitors Act 1974 allows solicitors to keep the interest earned on client money placed on general deposit.

Sample questions

Question 1

A firm of solicitors receives £250,000 on behalf of a client and pays it into the firm's general client account. The firm transfers the money to a separate designated deposit bank account (SDDBA).

Which of the following best explains why the firm made the transfer?

A Because the bank will calculate the interest payable on the SDDBA.

B Because the firm is not required to keep any accounting records for money held in a SDDBA.

C Because the money will be safer in a SDDBA.

D Because the SRA Solicitors' Accounts Rules require the money to be held in a SDDBA.

E Because the firm is entitled to keep all the interest earned on a SDDBA.

Answer

Option A is correct. There is no requirement under the Rules to place the money in a SDDBA (option D is therefore wrong). In these circumstances a firm would usually choose to open a SDDBA because it is administratively easier as the bank will calculate the real interest earned on the account. Option B is wrong; the firm is still required to keep accounting records on the money held in a SDDBA. Option E is wrong; the firm must account to the client for a fair sum by way of interest (Rule 7.1) and in practice the client would receive all the interest earned on the SDDBA. Option C is wrong as there is no greater security in money being held in a SDDBA.

Question 2

A solicitor is acting for a client in a business transaction. The solicitor receives £100,000 from the client to be used in the transaction. The solicitor pays the money into the firm's general client account. Unexpectedly, completion of the transaction is delayed, and the money is held in the general client account for much longer than anticipated. In view of the delay, the solicitor decides to allow £50 in interest.

Which of the following pair of double entries shows how the interest owed to the client should be recorded?

A CR Interest payable ledger account (Business section)
DR Client ledger account (Business section)

B DR Client ledger account (Client section)
CR Cash account (Client section)

C DR Interest payable ledger account (Business section)
CR Client ledger account (Client section)

D DR Client ledger account (Business section)
CR Cash account (Business section)

E DR Interest payable ledger account (Business section)
CR Client ledger account (Business section)

Answer

Option E is correct. When money is held in the general client account the interest payment is an expense of the business and will be recorded on an interest payable ledger account. The corresponding CR entry on the business section of the client ledger account shows that the firm owes £50 to the client.

Question 3

A firm received £200,000 on behalf of a client and paid the money into a separate designated deposit bank account. The bank informs the firm that £100 interest has been earned on the money.

Which of the following best describes how the firm should deal with the interest?

A Instruct the bank to transfer the interest to the firm's business bank account.

B Record the interest on the deposit section of the client's ledger account.

C Instruct the bank to transfer the interest to the client's ledger account.

D Record the interest on the business section of the client's ledger account.

E Record the interest on an interest payable ledger account.

Answer

Option B is correct. Interest earned on client money in a separate designated deposit bank account must be recorded on the client's ledger account. As it is the client's money it will be recorded in the deposit section (and not the business section - option D is wrong). Options A and C are wrong as the bank has no control over the ledgers maintained by the firm. Option E is wrong. An interest payable ledger account would be relevant if the firm was allowing a sum in lieu of interest on money held in the firm's general client bank account, but these are not the facts here.

8 Property Transactions

SQE1 syllabus

This chapter will help you to achieve the SQE1 Assessment Specification in relation to Functioning Legal Knowledge concerned with the core principles of double entry bookkeeping and the SRA Accounts Rules on:

- requirement to maintain accurate records;
- requirement to pay client money into a client account;
- withdrawals;
- transfers; and
- accounting entries required.

Note that for SQE1, candidates are not usually required to recall specific case names or cite statutory or regulatory authorities.

Learning outcomes

By the end of this chapter you will be able to apply relevant core principles of double entry bookkeeping and the SRA Accounts Rules appropriately and effectively, at the level of a competent newly qualified solicitor in practice, to realistic client-based ethical problems and situations in the following area:

- Particular property transactions.

8.1 Introduction

A common situation in which solicitors handle client money is when acting in the sale or purchase of a property. The solicitor must record all receipts and payments of client money for each client in accordance with the Rules. However, the nature of property transactions is such that they require particular care in terms of identifying who the money is being held for. Throughout the transaction the solicitor must consider carefully which client the firm is holding money for, and where money ceases to be held for one client and becomes held for someone else as this will require an inter-client transfer.

This chapter looks at:

- stakeholder money;
- bridging finance;
- mortgages.

8.2 Stakeholder money

When acting for the seller of a property, a firm may receive a deposit to hold as stakeholder. This is clearly a receipt of client money and so must be held in the client bank account. However, the firm is holding the money jointly for the buyer and the seller. It will not become the property of the seller unless and until completion takes place. Therefore, the firm cannot simply record the stakeholder money as held for the seller alone. (Note, however, that it is normal for conditions of sale to provide that sellers who are buying a residence in England and Wales may use all or any part of a deposit to fund the deposit on the property being purchased. See *Standard Conditions of Sale*, 5th edn, SC 2.2.5.)

The Guidance to Accountants issued by The Law Society on 16 December 2005 said that stakeholder money may be shown on the seller's ledger but must be clearly labelled as stakeholder money held for both buyer and seller. The current Rules do not say anything specific about stakeholder money. Rule 8.1 requires all receipts and payments of client money to be recorded in client ledgers identified by the client's name and an appropriate description of the matter to which they relate. This suggests that separate ledger accounts are required. However, the SRA has confirmed in correspondence that the Rules allow firms to manage their client accounts in a way that suits them, provided that client money remains protected and a clear audit trail shows the movement of money. It is, therefore, permissible to show stakeholder money on the seller's ledger account so long as it is labelled appropriately. For example:

DR Cash CR Seller's ledger account, noting money held as stakeholder	} Client section

Alternatively, the firm can have a separate stakeholder ledger account in the joint names of the client and the buyer and credit the stakeholder money to that account.

DR Cash CR Joint stakeholder ledger account	} Client section

As soon as completion takes place, the firm holds the money for the seller alone. This must be recorded by making an inter-client transfer from the joint stakeholder ledger account to the seller's ledger account.

On the day of completion:

DR Joint stakeholder ledger account CR Seller's ledger account	} Client section

This is more complicated than following the procedure suggested in the Guidance to Accountants. However, it has the advantage of keeping the entries relating to the stakeholder funds entirely separate from those relating to the money held for the seller alone. It therefore avoids the risk of making a payment from the client bank account for the seller using funds which are not yet available to the seller.

A deposit received as agent for the seller belongs to the seller alone and is credited directly to the seller's ledger account.

DR Cash	} Client section
CR Seller's ledger account	

8.3 Bridging finance

A deposit received as stakeholder is not available to the seller until completion without agreement (see, for example, *Standard Conditions of Sale* (5th edn), SC 2.2.5). A seller who is purchasing a replacement property may have insufficient cash available to pay the deposit on the purchase. Where a deposit is not available or is insufficient, it is possible to take a bridging loan from a bank to cover the period from exchange of contracts on the purchase to completion of the sale, when cash will become available.

A bridging loan is a personal loan to the borrower and, once received, belongs to the borrower and not the bank. Hence, when a solicitor receives the cash (whether direct from the bank or via the borrower), it will be held to the order of the borrower and must be credited to the borrower's ledger account, not to a ledger account in the name of the lending bank.

On completion of the sale, the loan, together with interest, must be repaid to the bank.

8.4 Mortgages

Many clients who buy property need to borrow money on mortgage. A client who sells property which is subject to a mortgage will have to redeem, ie repay, that mortgage after completion.

If a solicitor is acting for a client who is buying a property, the solicitor may also act for the lender, provided that there is no conflict of interest.

Where a solicitor is instructed to act for both the borrower and the lender, there are two separate clients. The solicitor must be clear for which client money is being held.

8.4.1 Mortgage advances – acting for buyer and lender

Money received from a lender as a mortgage advance is normally held for the lender until the day of completion.

Rule 8.1 requires receipts and payments of client money to be recorded on client ledgers identified by the client's name and an appropriate description of the matter. This requires separate ledgers for each client. The previous Rules contained a specific exception for loans from institutional lenders that provide mortgages on standard terms as part of their normal activities. Firms were allowed to credit the mortgage funds to the borrower's ledger account provided it was clearly labelled. Rule 8.1 has no exceptions but the SRA has confirmed in correspondence that the new rules allow firms to manage their client accounts in a way that suits them, provided that client money remains protected and a clear audit trail shows the movement of money.

Firms that act for both lender and borrower on the same matter can therefore choose how to treat mortgage funds:

Method 1

The mortgage advance is credited to the borrower's ledger account, when received. The details column must include the name of the lender and the fact that it is a mortgage advance.

Method 2

The mortgage advance is credited to a separate ledger account in the name of the lender on receipt. On the day of completion, the funds become available to the borrower, so an inter-client transfer should be made to the borrower's ledger account.

Method 1 is simpler but Method 2 gives a clearer audit trail.

Example

The Southern Cross Building Society advances £50,000 to Sharma on 6 June for his house purchase. Completion takes place on 8 June.

Method 1

Client: Sharma **Matter: House Purchase**		**Business account**			**Client account**		
Date	**Details**	**DR**	**CR**	**BAL**	**DR**	**CR**	**BAL**
June 6	Cash. Southern Cross Building Society. Mortgage advance					50,000	50,000CR

Method 2

Client: Southern Cross **Matter: Mortgage Advance. Sharma**		**Business account**			**Client account**		
Date	**Details**	**DR**	**CR**	**BAL**	**DR**	**CR**	**BAL**
June 6	Cash. Mortgage advance. Sharma					50,000	50,000CR
8	Sharma. Transfer				50,000		—

Client: Sharma **Matter: House Purchase**		**Business account**			**Client account**		
Date	**Details**	**DR**	**CR**	**BAL**	**DR**	**CR**	**BAL**
June 8	Southern Cross. Mortgage. Transfer					50,000	50,000CR

Frequently, the money advanced by way of mortgage will be paid direct to the seller's solicitor by the lender. In such a case, as the buyer's solicitor does not handle the mortgage advance, there will be no entries relating to the money in the accounts of the buyer's solicitor.

8.4.2 Professional charges on mortgage advance

The firm is entitled to charge the lender for work done in connection with the mortgage advance as well as to charge the buyer for the work done in connection with the purchase. The buyer will frequently have agreed with the lender to pay the costs charged to the lender. The normal rule is that costs and VAT must be debited to the ledger account of the person (Person A) to whom the legal services were supplied. If another person, B, is discharging the debt by way of indemnity, the debt can be transferred from A's ledger account to B's ledger account.

DR Buyer's ledger account, business section with fees charged on the purchase and VAT

CR Profit costs account and HMRC account with the fees and VAT

DR Lender's ledger account, business section with fees charged on the mortgage and VAT

CR Profit costs account and HMRC account with the fees and VAT

Transfer debt from the lender's ledger account to the borrower's ledger account:

CR Lender's ledger account, business section with fees charged on the mortgage and VAT as one figure

DR Buyer's ledger account, business section with fees charged on the purchase and VAT as one figure

If the firm has chosen not to have a separate ledger account for the lender, the charges and VAT of the lender will have to be shown on the borrower's ledger account.

Example

On 8 June the firm charges Southern Cross £120 + £24 VAT for acting for it on the mortgage advance. Sharma has agreed to pay the charges. The firm charges Sharma £200 + £40 VAT for acting on the purchase.

Method 1

Client: Sharma **Matter: House Purchase**		**Business account**			**Client account**		
Date	**Details**	**DR**	**CR**	**BAL**	**DR**	**CR**	**BAL**
June							
6	Cash. Southern Cross Building Society. Mortgage advance.					50,000	50,000CR
8	Profit costs	200		200DR			
	VAT	40		240DR			
8	Profit costs. Southern Cross. Mortgage advance	120		360DR			
	VAT	24		384DR			

Method 2

Client: Southern Cross Matter: Mortgage Advance. Sharma		Business account			Client account		
Date	Details	DR	CR	BAL	DR	CR	BAL
June							
6	Cash. Mortgage advance. Sharma					50,000	50,000CR
8	Sharma. Transfer				50,000		—
8	Profit costs	120		120DR			
	VAT	24		144DR			
8	Sharma. Costs. Transfer		144	—			

Client: Sharma Matter: House Purchase		Business account			Client account		
Date	Details	DR	CR	BAL	DR	CR	BAL
June							
8	Southern Cross. Mortgage. Transfer					50,000	50,000CR
8	Profit costs	200		200DR			
	VAT	40		240DR			
8	Southern Cross. Costs. Transfer	144		384DR			

8.4.3 Mortgage redemption – acting for lender and seller

Many sellers have a balance left on their mortgage at the date of sale. The balance has to be paid off from the proceeds of sale.

It is uncommon to act for both lender and seller. However, it is possible. Where this is the case, some of the sale proceeds will be received for the seller and some for the lender. The whole of the receipt is client money and will be paid into the client bank account. In order to comply with the requirements of Rule 8.1 the firm will need to show who it is holding the client money for.

The clearest audit trail would be to credit the whole amount to the seller's ledger account initially, to give a full picture of the sums handled for the seller. The firm would then do an immediate inter-client transfer of the amount required to redeem the mortgage.

CR Seller's ledger account DR Cash account	} Client section
DR Seller's ledger account CR Lender's ledger account	} Client section

The firm will then pay the mortgage redemption money to the lender.

DR Lender's ledger account } Client section
CR Cash account

As an alternative the firm can take a more streamlined approach and split the credit entries at the time of receipt. If this is done, the firm will credit part of the proceeds to the seller's ledger account and part to the lender's ledger account. The whole amount is debited to the cash account client section.

8.4.4 Professional charges on mortgage redemption

The seller may have agreed to pay the legal fees of the lender. The seller's solicitor will address a bill to the lender. The legal fees on the mortgage redemption must initially be debited to the lender's ledger account. The debt will then be transferred to the seller's ledger account to show that it is the seller who will discharge it, not the lender.

DR Seller's ledger account, business section, with fees charged on the sale and VAT

CR Profit costs account and HMRC account with fees charged on the sale and VAT

DR Lender's ledger account, business section, with fees charged on the mortgage and VAT

CR Profit costs account and HMRC account with fees charged on the mortgage and VAT

Transfer debt from the lender's ledger account to the seller's ledger account:

CR Lender's ledger account with fees charged on the mortgage and VAT as one amount

DR Seller's ledger account with fees charged on the mortgage and VAT as one amount

Summary

- If a firm has been holding client money for one client and then starts to hold some or all of it for another client, the firm must open a client ledger account for the transferee and record an inter-client transfer of the money.
- A deposit received as stakeholder is client money and must be paid into the client bank account. It is held for the buyer and seller jointly so it must be credited to a joint leger account (usually called 'stakeholder'). It is possible to credit the deposit to the seller's ledger account with a note identifying it as stakeholder money held jointly for the seller and buyer. On the day the sale is completed the cash becomes the seller's. The firm must make an inter-client transfer to show that the deposit is now held for the seller alone.
- Where a mortgage advance is received, the money is client money and must be paid into the client bank account. It should be credited to the ledger account for the lender.

Sample questions

Question 1

A solicitor is acting for the seller of a property. The terms of the contract provide for the buyer to pay a 10% deposit on exchange of contracts to be held by the seller's solicitor as stakeholder. On exchange of contracts the solicitor receives the 10% deposit.

Which of the following best describes how the solicitor should deal with the deposit?

A Pay the money into the firm's client bank account but make no ledger entries to record the receipt.

B Pay the money into the firm's business bank account and record the receipt on the stakeholder ledger account in the joint names of buyer and seller.

C Forward the money to the seller and record the receipt on the stakeholder ledger account in the joint names of buyer and seller.

D Pay the money into the firm's client bank account and record the receipt on the stakeholder ledger account in the joint names of buyer and seller.

E Pay the money into the firm's business bank account and record the receipt on the seller's client ledger account.

Answer

Option D is correct. This is a receipt of client money (Rule 2.1(b)) and so it must be paid into the firm's client bank account. A receipt of client money must be recorded (Rule 8.1). Stakeholder money is held jointly for seller and buyer and therefore the best option is to record the receipt on a separate stakeholder ledger account in the joint names of buyer and seller. (It is also permissible to record the entry on the seller's ledger account, but labelled as stakeholder money held for both buyer and seller.)

Question 2

A firm is acting for a client in the purchase of a property. The client pays the firm £400,000 to use in part payment of the purchase price of £500,000. The client will fund the balance of the purchase price by borrowing £100,000 from a building society by way of a mortgage. The firm is also acting for the lender in relation to the mortgage.

Prior to completion of the purchase, the firm receives the mortgage advance and pays the money into the firm's client bank account. The firm records the receipt on a client ledger account in the name of the lender.

Which of the following best describes the accounting records the firm should make on the borrower's ledger account on completion?

A An inter-client transfer of £100,000 from the lender's ledger account followed by a payment of £500,000 to the seller.

B A payment of £500,000 to the seller.

C A payment of £400,000 to the seller.

D An inter-client transfer of £400,000 to the lender's ledger account.

E An inter-client transfer of £500,000 from the lender's ledger account followed by a payment of £500,000 to the seller.

Answer

Option A is correct. On receipt of the mortgage advance, the mortgage money was held by the firm on behalf of the lender. On completion the mortgage money is now held for the borrower and this must be recorded by first making an inter-client transfer. The firm will then record the payment of the whole purchase price to the seller on the borrower's ledger account.

9 Joint Accounts, the Client's Own Bank Account and Third Party Managed Accounts

SQE1 syllabus

This chapter will enable you to achieve the SQE1 Assessment Specification in relation to Functioning Legal Knowledge concerned with the core principles of double entry bookkeeping and the SRA Accounts Rules on:

- the operation of joint accounts;
- the operation of a client's own account;
- third party managed accounts.

Note that for SQE1, candidates are not usually required to recall specific case names or cite statutory or regulatory authorities.

Learning outcomes

By the end of this chapter you will be able to apply relevant core principles of double entry bookkeeping and the SRA Accounts Rules appropriately and effectively, at the level of a competent newly qualified solicitor in practice, to realistic client-based ethical problems and situations in the following areas:

- The requirements when operating a joint account;
- The requirements when acting as a signatory on the client's own account;
- The possible benefits of using third party managed accounts;
- Dealing with the SRA and the client when using a TPMA.

9.1 Introduction

When a solicitor has any involvement with other people's money it will usually be client money passing through the client bank account. However, it is possible for a solicitor to engage in dealings with money which belongs to a client or a third party but which for some reason does not fall within the definition of client money and/or is properly held somewhere other than the client bank account.

This chapter looks at:

- SRA Principles and Code of Conduct;
- joint accounts;
- operating a client's own account;
- third party managed accounts.

9.2 SRA Principles and Code of Conduct

In any dealings with money belonging to a client or a third party a solicitor is subject to some core duties. SRA Principle 7 requires that a solicitor must act in the client's best interests. Paragraph 4.2 of the SRA Code of Conduct for Solicitors, RELs and RFLs requires a solicitor to take steps to safeguard money or assets entrusted to the solicitor by clients and others.

9.3 Joint accounts

A solicitor or a firm may open a joint account with a client or third party. A typical example is where a solicitor, who is a joint executor named in a will, is dealing with the administration of the estate. The nature of the account is that both joint account holders can pay money into, withdraw money from and generally manage the account.

The account will be in the joint names of the solicitor/firm and the client or third party. As the account is not in the name of the solicitor/firm alone it is not a client account. Consequently, those elements of the Rules concerned with client accounts do not apply to a joint account. The money held in the account is nevertheless client money.

Rules 2–8 do not apply to money held in a joint account save for (by virtue of Rule 9.1):

(a) obtaining statements from banks and building societies and other financial institutions at least every five weeks (Rule 8.2); and

(b) keeping a readily accessible central record of bills and other notifications of costs (Rule 8.4).

The fact that the other joint account holder has access to money in the account could present an added risk. Bearing in mind the need to safeguard money entrusted by clients and others (SRA Code of Conduct for Solicitors, RELs and RFLs, Paragraph 4.2) it may be necessary for the solicitor to take additional steps to minimise the risk, eg ensuring that the account operates on joint signatures only.

9.4 Operating a client's own account

It is sometimes the case that a solicitor or firm will operate the client's own personal bank account as a signatory. A typical example is where the solicitor has a power of attorney over the client's financial affairs or where the solicitor has been appointed as a deputy by the court of protection to deal with the financial affairs of a vulnerable person.

When operating a client's own bank account, the client's money will not pass through the firm's bank accounts. Instead the solicitor will be making payments directly from and receiving money directly into the client's own bank account.

As the account is in the name of the client rather than the solicitor/firm it is not a client account. The money held in the account may or may not be client money depending on the circumstances. For example, if the solicitor is holding the money as a trustee then it will fall within the definition of client money (Rule 2.1(c)).

Rules 2–8 do not apply to money held in a client's own account such money save for (by virtue of Rule 10.1):

(a) obtaining statements from banks and building societies and other financial institutions at least every five weeks (Rule 8.2);

(b) completing reconciliations of the account at least every five weeks (Rule 8.3); and

(b) keeping a readily accessible central record of bills and other notifications of costs (Rule 8.4).

It may be the case that a solicitor does not have such frequent and regular access to bank/building society statements to be able to carry out reconciliations every five weeks. If a solicitor is unable to meet these requirements, the SRA's position is that it will not consider the solicitor to be in breach of Rule 10 provided the solicitor has taken reasonable steps to satisfy themselves that the client's money is not at risk and recorded the position appropriately.

In its current consultation on minor amendments to the Standards and Regulations, the SRA reported that firms operating a client's own account have reported difficulty in implementing the requirements to reconcile client accounts every five weeks and obtain bank statements. Many firms reported that it is often not possible to access monthly bank statements to an account belonging to a client which they control. The SRA therefore proposed to amend Rule 10 in order to make the arrangements workable so that firms must:

- undertake reconciliation every 16 weeks;
- maintain a central register of clients' own accounts under control of the firm;
- keep records of transactions carried out by the firm on behalf of the client and record bills and other notification of costs relating to the client's matter.

The proposal adds a new Rule 10.2 requiring the reconciliation to be signed off by the COFA or a manager of the firm at least every 16 weeks. However, as with the other proposed amendments to the Rules, this has been postponed pending the SRA's wider review.

9.5 Third party managed accounts

Rule 11.1 allows firms to enter an agreement with a client to use a third party managed account (TPMA) to hold client money, rather than operating the firm's own client bank account.

Money held in a TPMA is not held or received by the solicitor but by the TPMA provider. Consequently, it does not come within the definition of client money. Therefore, it does not have to be held in accordance with those of the SRA Accounts Rules dealing with the holding of client money.

SRA Guidance 'Third Party Managed Accounts' makes it clear that, in order to comply with the obligations to act in the client's best interests and safeguard a client's money, both the decision to use a TPMA and the selection of the particular TPMA must be appropriate in each individual case.

Although using a TPMA comes with some costs, it can reduce overall firm overheads, especially if the firm only occasionally holds client money. For example, outsourcing the holding of client money can reduce professional indemnity insurance premiums and contributions to the Compensation Fund, Accountants' reports also do not need to be prepared.

There are potential benefits beyond cost savings. Although it is impossible to eliminate all risk related to cybercrime, TPMAs could be a more secure way of handling a client's money. Using a TPMA may also help address a firm's money laundering risk.

As part of its consultation on client money in legal services, the SRA has put forward the controversial proposal that the use of TPMAs should replace the model of using client bank accounts to hold client money.

9.5.1 The TPMA provider and the TPMA

In the Guidance referred to above, the SRA states that it expects firms to make sure that the TPMA provider is regulated by the Financial Conduct Authority (FCA). The TPMA provider must be:

- an authorised payment institution;
- a small payment institution which has adopted voluntary safeguarding arrangements to the same level as an authorised payment institution; or
- an EEA authorised payment institution.

The TPMA must be an account held at a bank or building society by which the third party receives and pays out money on the solicitor's and the client's behalf (an escrow payment service).

9.5.2 Engaging with the client

The fundamental requirement under Paragraph 8.6 of the SRA Code of Conduct for Solicitors, RELs and RFLs is that clients must be given information in a way that they can understand and are in a position to make informed decisions. In the context of a TPMA this means that the client must understand how their money will be held and how the transaction will work.

In addition, a firm entering into arrangements with a client to use a TPMA on behalf of the client must take reasonable steps to ensure, before accepting instructions, that the client is informed of and understands:

(a) the terms of the contractual arrangements relating to the use of the third party managed account, and in particular how any fees for use of the third party managed account will be paid and who will bear them (Rule 11.1(b)(i)); and

(b) the client's right to terminate the agreement and dispute payment requests made by the firm (Rule 11.1(b)(ii)).

9.5.3 Operating the TPMA

By definition, operating the TPMA falls to the third party. However, the solicitor must nevertheless maintain an overview of the transactions on the account and keep appropriate records to reflect this. In particular the solicitor must obtain regular statements from the provider and ensure that these accurately reflect all the transactions on the account (Rule 11.2).

In order to comply with Rule 2.1 of the SRA Code of Conduct for Firms, it will be necessary for a firm to have its own internal systems in place for monitoring the operation of the TPMA.

9.5.4 Regulatory protection

The fact that the TPMA is regulated by the FCA affords the client regulatory protection. The protection will different to that of the SRA where money is held in an ordinary client account. The client must be made aware of that difference (Paragraph 8.11 Code of Conduct for Solicitors, RELs and RFLs). For example, the client should be told that complaints about the TPMA provider should be made to the provider and in accordance with the provider's complaints procedure.

9.5.5 SRA Guidance

A firm does not need permission from the SRA to use a TPMA. However, in the Guidance referred to above, the SRA says that it does expect firms to notify it, using its TPMA form. The form asks for the following information:

- the name and SRA number of the firm;
- the name of the TPMA provider;
- the TPMA provider's FCA authorisation number; and
- the date on which the plans to start using a TPMA as part of its business.

If the same TPMA provider is used for several clients, it is only necessary to inform the SRA the first time that the TPMA provider is used. If more than one TPMA provider is used, the SRA expects to be notified of all providers.

Summary

- When dealing with money belonging to a client or a third party a solicitor is bound by the rules of professional conduct including the duty to act in the client's best interests (SRA Principle 7) and the requirement to safeguard money entrusted to the solicitor (Paragraph 4.2 of the SRA Code of Conduct for Solicitors, RELs and RFLs).
- Money may sometimes be held in an account in the joint names of the solicitor/firm and a client or third party. Such an arrangement is subject to the requirements to obtain regular statements and keep a central record of bills.
- A solicitor may be a signatory on the client's personal bank account. The solicitor will be subject to the requirements to obtain regular statements, complete reconciliations and keep a central record of bills.
- A firm can dispense with holding a client bank account by using a TPMA.
- The SRA must be informed when a firm decides to use a TPMA provider and the client fully informed of the arrangement.

Sample question

A solicitor is a joint executor named in a will. The solicitor is now dealing with the administration of the estate. To assist with the administration the solicitor opens a bank account. The solicitor is one signatory on the account. The second signatory is the other executor named in the will.

Which of the following best explains the solicitor's obligations with regard to the money held in the bank account?

A Because the money is not being held in a client account, the solicitor must safeguard the money, but has no obligations under the SRA Accounts Rules.

B Because this is not client money, the solicitor is not subject to the SRA Accounts Rules.

C Because the money is being held in a joint account, the solicitor's only obligations are to obtain bank statements on the account every five weeks and keep a central record of bills.

D Because the money is not being held in a client account, the solicitor has limited obligations under the SRA Accounts Rules but must still safeguard the money.

E Because this is client money, the SRA Accounts Rules apply in their entirety.

Answer

Option D is correct. The money is being held in a joint account. This does not fall within the definition of a client account, but the money is nevertheless client money. As it is not a client account, only limited elements of the Rules apply. A solicitor entrusted with money is always under a duty to safeguard that money (SRA Code of Conduct for Solicitors, RELs and RFLs, para 4.2), so in addition to Rules 8.2 (obtain five-weekly bank statements) and 8.4 (keep a record of bills) of the SRA Accounts Rules, the solicitor may need to take additional steps to minimise the risk.

10 Compliance

SQE1 syllabus

This chapter will enable you to achieve the SQE1 Assessment Specification in relation to Functioning Legal Knowledge concerned with the core principles of double entry bookkeeping and the SRA Accounts Rules on:

- accountants' reports;
- storage and retention of accounting records.

Note that for SQE1, candidates are not usually required to recall specific case names or cite statutory or regulatory authorities.

Learning outcomes

By the end of this chapter you will be able to apply relevant core principles of double entry bookkeeping and the SRA Accounts Rules appropriately and effectively, at the level of a competent newly qualified solicitor in practice, to realistic client-based ethical problems and situations in the following areas:

- The investigative powers of the SRA;
- The requirements in relation to accountants' reports.

10.1 Introduction

The primary purpose of the SRA Accounts Rules is to keep client money safe. The SRA needs to be satisfied that firms and individuals are acting in compliance with the Rules and, if not, that breaches are brought to its attention and the appropriate action taken. To that end the SRA may require a firm's accounts to be inspected periodically by an independent accountant to assess compliance with the Rules.

The SRA takes a targeted approach to the need to obtain and submit an accountants' report. Solicitors' practices that present little or no risk (such as those firms that do not hold much client money) are exempt from obtaining a report from their accountant and only qualified reports are required to be submitted to the SRA.

This chapter looks at:

- accountants' reports;
- the retention and storage of accounting records.

10.2 Accountants' reports

Rule 12.1 provides that firms which have, at any time during an accounting period, held or received client money, or operated a joint account or a client's own account as signatory, must obtain an accountant's report for that accounting period within six months of the end of the period. A failure to obtain an accountant's report where one is required is considered a serious regulatory matter by the SRA.

The purpose of the report is for the accountant to confirm compliance (or otherwise) with the Rules. The accountant will use their professional judgement in determining what investigations need to be carried out and assessing compliance with the Rules. Accountants are under a separate duty under the Solicitors Act 1974 to immediately report to the SRA any evidence of theft or fraud or where there are concerns about whether a solicitor or firm is fit and proper to hold money for clients or third parties.

The report must be delivered to the SRA within six months of the end of the accounting period if it is qualified to show a failure to comply with the Rules, such that money belonging to clients or third parties is, or has been, or is likely to be placed, at risk. The obligation to submit the report lies with the firm and its managers, not with the reporting accountant (although in practice reporting accountants can and do submit reports to the SRA). In the past all accountants' reports had to be submitted to the SRA, not just those reports which were subject to qualifications. As part of its consultation on client money in legal services, the SRA is considering reintroducing the requirement for all firms holding client money to submit their accountant's report.

The SRA guidance, 'Planning for and completing an accountant's report' (14 September 2020), says:

> We do not consider it appropriate to strictly define when a report must be qualified. We will rely on the accountant's professional judgement to assess the firm's compliance with the Accounts Rules and whether money belonging to clients or third parties, is, has been or may be placed at risk. We would expect an assessment to be based on an understanding of the seriousness of all the risks posed in the context of the firm's size and complexity, areas of work, systems and controls, compliance history and the likely impact on the firm and its clients if money were to be misused or not accounted for.

However, it does give some examples of 'Serious factors' – the presence of one or more of which is likely to lead to a qualification – and 'Moderate factors' – the presence of one or more of which may lead to a qualification depending on context (including factors such as the number of instances, whether the firm identified the breaches and what corrective action, if any, has been taken as a consequence).

Serious factors include:

- A significant and/or unreplaced shortfall (including client debit balances or business credit balances) on client account, including client money held elsewhere, for example a client's own account, unless caused by bank error and rectified promptly.
- Systematic billing for fees and any disbursements that have not been incurred and payments in respect of that bill being made into the business account.
- Evidence of any disregard for the safety of client money and assets.
- Actual or suspected fraud or dishonesty by the managers or employees of the firm (that may impact upon the safety of money belonging to clients or third parties).
- Accounting records not available or significantly deficient or bank accounts/ledgers failing to include reference to a client (Rules 8.1, 8.2 and 8.3).
- A failure to provide documentation requested by the reporting accountant (Rule 12.8).
- Client account bank reconciliations not carried out.
- The client account is improperly used as a banking facility (Rule 3.3). Please refer to our Warning Notice on this and associated case studies.

Rule 12.2 provides that firms are not required to obtain an accountant's report if:

(a) all of the client money held or received during an accounting period is money received from the Legal Aid Agency; or

(b) in the accounting period, the total balance of all client accounts plus any joint accounts and clients' own accounts operated by the firm does not exceed:

    (i) an average of £10,000; and

    (ii) a maximum of £250,000,

    or the equivalent in foreign currency.

Where a firm ceases to practise as an authorised body regulated by the SRA and to hold or operate a client account, or the SRA considers that it is otherwise in the public interest to do so, the SRA may require it to obtain or deliver an accountant's report to the SRA on reasonable notice (Rule 12.4). The effect of Rule 12.4 is that the SRA will only require firms to submit a final report when a firm shuts down and closes its client account on a case-by-case basis, if it believes that it is necessary.

Any report obtained must be prepared and signed by an accountant who is a member of one of the chartered accountancy bodies and who is, or works for, a registered auditor.

Rule 12.6 provides that the SRA may disqualify an accountant from preparing a report for the purposes of this rule if:

(a) the accountant has been found guilty by their professional body of professional misconduct or equivalent; or

(b) the SRA is satisfied that the accountant has failed to exercise due care and skill in the preparation of a report under these Rules.

Rule 12.8 provides that firms must provide the accountant preparing a report with the following:

(a) details of all accounts held at any bank, building society or other financial institution at any time during the accounting period to which the report relates; and

(b) all other information and documentation that the accountant requires to enable completion of their report.

10.3 Retention and storage of accounting records

All accounting records should be securely stored and retained for at least six years (Rule 13.1).

The term 'accounting records' is widely defined in the Glossary to include, for example, reconciliations, bank statements, electronic records, accountants' reports, and documents relating to third party managed accounts.

Summary

- With some limited exceptions the accounts of firms that have held or received client money or operated a joint account or a client's own account as signatory, must be inspected by an accountant within six months of the end of the accounting period.
- The inspecting accountant will prepare a report confirming, or otherwise, compliance with the Rules.
- An accountant's report which is qualified to show a failure to comply with the Rules, such that money belonging to clients or third parties is, or has been, or is likely to be placed, at risk must be submitted to the SRA.
- A firm must securely store and retain its accounting records for at least six years.

Sample question

A firm of solicitors was set up 14 months ago. During its first accounting year the firm has generally handled only small amounts of client money, but on three occasions the balance on the firm's client bank account has exceeded £1m.

Which of the following best describes the firm's obligations with regard to obtaining an accountant's report?

A The firm is not obliged to obtain an accountant's report because it only handles small amounts of client money.

B The firm is not obliged to obtain an accountant's report because it is only at the end of its first accounting year.

C The firm must obtain an accountant's report, but only needs to submit the report to the SRA if it is qualified.

D The firm must obtain an accountant's report and must submit the report to the SRA even if it is not qualified.

E The firm must obtain an accountant's report and must submit the report to the SRA if it is not qualified but discloses a breach of the SRA Accounts Rules.

Answer

Option C is correct. Most firms have to obtain an accountant's report (with the result that options A and B do not represent the best answer), but only qualified reports (where there has been a significant breach of the Rules) need to be submitted to the SRA (options D and E therefore are wrong). Firms handling only small amounts of client money are not required to obtain a report but having a client bank account balance in excess of £250,000 (Rule 12.2(b)(ii)) during the accounting year takes the firm outside the exception.

Index